Science for All Seasons
Fall

Grades PreK-K

Project Manager:
Michele M. Dare

Writers:
Lucia Kemp Henry
Dr. Suzanne Moore

Editors:
Cindy K. Daoust, Ada Goren, Sherri Lynn Kuntz, Leanne Stratton

Art Coordinator:
Kimberly Richard

Artists:
Teresa Davidson, Theresa Lewis Goode, Nick Greenwood,
Sheila Krill, Rob Mayworth, Kimberly Richard,
Rebecca Saunders, Barry Slate

Cover Artists:
Nick Greenwood and Kimberly Richard

www.themailbox.com

©2000 by THE EDUCATION CENTER, INC.
All rights reserved.
ISBN #1-56234-384-X

Manufactured in the United States

10 9 8 7 6 5 4 3 2 1

Table of Contents

Fall Is in the Air

Cooler temperatures, warmer clothes, colorful leaves…it must be fall! Invite your little ones to study fall weather and the changes that signal this new season.

Looking for Fall

Even if the autumn changes in your area are subtle, your youngsters can find signs around them that say, "Fall is here!" Usher in the season by taking students for a walk outdoors to search for sights that signal the arrival of autumn. Prior to your excursion, make a copy of the "Fall Sights" record card on page 7 for each child. Staple each card to an individual piece of cardboard. Then give each child a crayon and a record card before you head outdoors. As you walk, encourage students to search their surroundings for signs of fall in the animals, clothing, trees, and weather around them. (If signs of fall are scarce in your area, enlarge the pictures from the card, color them, cut them apart, and place them along your walking trail for students to spot.) As each child sees an item pictured on her card, have her color the picture. At the end of your walk, return to your classroom for a discussion of this crisp and cool new season.

Let's Talk (and Sing) About Autumn

After your nature walk, lead a discussion about the fall sights your little ones saw. Display a large leaf shape cut from yellow bulletin board paper. Ask students to name the fall things they saw—both items that were on their "Fall Sights" cards and items that weren't. Write students' suggestions on the leaf shape to create a fall vocabulary list. Then teach little ones the tune below. As you repeat the verse, replace the underlined words with words and phrases from the list.

Later, invite youngsters to draw fall scenes, incorporating some of the things they listed on the leaf shape. Post the drawings and the leaf shape on a bulletin board.

Fall Is Here!

(sung to the tune of "Down by the Bay")

Oh, fall is here. It's everywhere!
We see the changes here and there.
Oh, we can see [the green leaves change].
Can you feel it everywhere? Fall is in the air!
Yes, fall is here!

acorns
colorful leaves
jackets   sweaters
yellow grass
chilly air
squirrels

Autumn Leaf Exploration

Little ones will jump at the chance to visit this discovery center! Set up a large kiddie pool on a painter's drop cloth inside your classroom. Half-fill the pool with fall leaves; then invite a small group of students to join you there. Encourage your young scientists to use their observation skills as they explore and talk about the leaves. Ask questions to stimulate students' thinking, such as the following: Where do you think these leaves came from? What do the leaves feel like? What colors do you see?

As the leaves become crushed, remove them. (They'll make wonderful mulch for a class garden!) Then put a new supply of leaves in the pool for further exploration.

Leaf Comparisons

Have youngsters take a look at leaves to sharpen their comparison skills. In advance, find two leaves of the same size from a maple, oak, or other deciduous tree. Choose one that is mostly green and one that has changed to its fall color. (Or cut matching leaf shapes from green and red paper.) Ask students to tell you how the two leaves are alike (size and shape) and how they are different (color). If desired, repeat the process with other pairs of leaves. Later, place a pile of real or paper leaves in a center for little ones to sort and compare.

Did You Know?

In fall, the weather gets cooler and we have fewer hours of sunlight. The change in the amount of light tells deciduous trees that winter is approaching. Winter is a time of rest for these trees, and their leaves don't need the *chlorophyll* that helps them absorb sunlight and make food for the tree. The chlorophyll in leaves gives them their green color. So as the chlorophyll disappears, so does the green color, revealing the bright colors we associate with fall.

Here Are the Leaves

Teach your little leaf lovers this fall fingerplay to reinforce the seasonal changes in deciduous trees.

Here are the leaves up on the tree,	*Hold hands up, palms out.*
Just as green as they can be.	*Nod head.*
Here comes fall. The air gets cold.	*Wrap arms around body; shiver.*
The green leaves change to red and gold.	*Hold hands up, palms out.*
Here come the leaves, tumbling down...	*Wave hands and arms.*
No leaves on the tree.	*Point up.*
They're all on the ground!	*Point down.*

Frosty Observations

Have your youngsters spied frost on leaves, on the ground, or on car windows on a cold autumn morning? Try this experiment to demonstrate how fall's chilly temperatures cause frost to form. You'll need two identical clear drinking glasses and access to a freezer. To begin, set the two empty glasses on a table for students to observe. Point out that the glasses are identical and that both are empty. Leave one on the table and have youngsters watch as you place the other glass in the freezer. After 30 minutes or more, remove the glass from the freezer and set it next to the glass on the table. Encourage students to touch and compare the outside surfaces of both glasses; then have them speculate on why the glass from the freezer is covered with frost. Lead students to conclude that the cold temperature in the freezer caused the frost to form.

This Is Why

Frost forms when water vapor changes directly to a solid. The glass in the freezer becomes cold enough to cause the water vapor in the air around it to cool very quickly. This rapid cooling changes the water vapor touching the surface of the glass into tiny ice crystals.

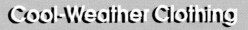

Long Sleeves	Short Sleeves
Lynn (name)	Keiko (name)
Karim (name)	Todd (name)
Tim (name)	Glen (name)
Shelly (name)	
Scott (name)	

Cool-Weather Clothing

Invite your young weather wizards to collect some data about fall temperatures—it's as simple as having them check out the clothes they're wearing! To prepare, copy, cut out, and personalize a set of the shirt patterns on page 7 for each child. To begin the activity, direct students wearing long-sleeved shirts to line up on one side of your classroom; have students wearing short-sleeved shirts line up on the other side. Explain that as the weather gets cooler, people tend to wear warmer clothing, including shirts with long sleeves instead of short ones. Ask your group to compare the number of students in each line to decide whether the weather outdoors is likely to be cool or warm. Next, give each child a shirt pattern to match what she is wearing (long or short sleeves). Have her color the shirt and then attach it to a two-column graph. Count the shirts in each column and discuss students' impressions about the weather based on their clothing choices. Make a new graph each morning to involve your whole group in the daily weather report. Isn't it cool when every child is dressed for scientific success?

Teach little ones this tune about the chill of autumn. If desired, have youngsters brainstorm synonyms for "chilly" to substitute in the first and fourth lines.

(sung to the tune of "Shortnin' Bread")

In the fall the weather gets [chilly, chilly].
In the fall the temperature starts to drop.
Get out your sweater! Get out your hat!
The weather's getting [chilly] now;
That's a fact!

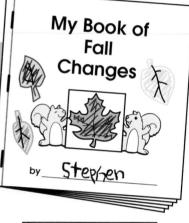

Fall Changes Booklet

Wrap up your exploration of fall weather by inviting each child to put together a festive booklet about the changes that take place in autumn. For each child, duplicate the booklet cover, patterns, and pages on construction paper. (See pages 8–12.) Use an X-acto® knife to cut out the circle on each student's copy of booklet page 4. Then read through the directions for completing the booklet and gather the necessary materials. Guide each child as he completes his booklet cover and pages; then help him sequence and staple his booklet together along the left side.

Cover: Cut out the cover. Color the leaf pattern, cut it out, and glue it to the page where indicated. Draw and color leaves around the title. Write your name.

Page 1: Cut out the page and the cloud pattern. Color the sky area on the page with a gray crayon. Glue the cloud to the page; then draw raindrops below the cloud with a blue glitter pen. Glue pieces of cotton ball to the cloud.

Page 2: Cut out the page. Color the tree trunk pattern, cut it out, and glue it to the page where indicated. Use a rubber stamp and an ink pad to decorate the tree with leaf shapes.

Page 3: Cut out the page. Color the moon pattern and cut it out. Color the sky area on the page with a gray crayon. Then glue the moon to the page. Draw a picture of yourself inside the house.

Page 4: Color the sweatshirt pattern; then cut it out. Glue the sweatshirt to the page where indicated. Draw leaves on the page. Tape a photocopy of your school photo to the back of the page so that your face shows through.

Fall Sights

seen by _____

Shirt Patterns
Use with "Cool-Weather Clothing" on page 5.

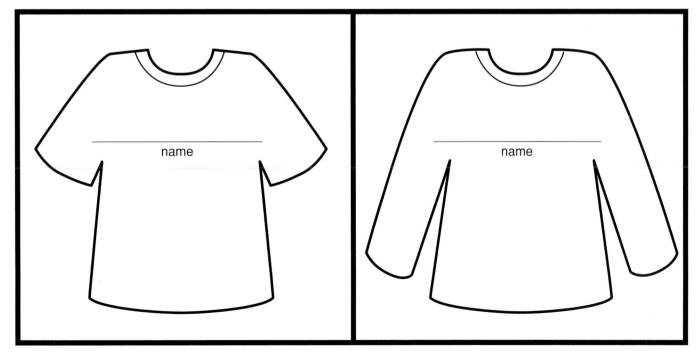

name

name

Booklet Cover

Use with "Fall Changes Booklet" on page 6.

My Book of Fall Changes

by _____

Color.

Cut.

Glue.

The weather changes. It gets colder.

brr!

1

Color.
Cut.
Glue.

Booklet Page 2
Use with "Fall Changes Booklet" on page 6.

Daylight changes. It gets dark early.

It's dark now!

3

Color.

Cut.

Glue.

Booklet Page 4

Use with "Fall Changes Booklet" on page 6.

The Green Scene

Seed Safari

All plants have some way to spread their seeds. Seeds stick, glide,
roll, and float. Where are they going? On a…seed safari!

Hitchhiking Seeds

Give your budding botanists a hands-on (and feet-on!)
experience with one form of seed travel. In advance, duplicate
the parent note on page 17 and fill in the desired date. Then
make a class supply. Several days prior to the activity, have
each student color, cut out, and personalize his note. Have
him glue it to a paper lunch bag and take the bag home.

On the appointed day, have each child slip his sock over
one of his shoes. (Be sure to have a few extra socks on
hand for children who forget theirs.) Invite youngsters to
take a walk through a grassy area outside—the drier, the
better. As they walk, they'll be collecting seeds on their
sock-covered feet. After returning to your classroom,
encourage each child to take a peek at his sock; there will
be plenty of seeds sticking to it! Ask youngsters to speculate
why the seeds are stuck to their socks. Then have each child
carefully remove his sock, and continue your study with the
activity described in "Take a Closer Look."

Dear Parent,
I am going on
a Seed Safari!
Please send
one adult-sized
thick sock
in this sack
by *Oct. 23*.
(date)

Kimberly
name

This Is Why

In nature, seeds must travel to a favorable spot in order
to sprout and grow. One of the ways seeds travel is by
sticking to clothing, animal fur, or bird feathers. Sticking
seeds have hooks, barbs, or spines that help them hitch a
ride to a new location. They may ride a long way
before falling to the ground.

Take a Closer Look

Now that your youngsters have collected some
seeds, it's time for an up-close inspection. Encourage each child to carefully pull the seeds off his
sock. Provide plastic magnifying glasses so your
little ones can get a good look at their seed specimens. Ask each child to sort his seeds by type.
What similarities and differences does he see?
Save some of the seeds your youngsters have
collected for "Water Travelers" on page 15. Then
extend this activity by planting some of the remaining seeds so your students can watch them sprout.

Thomas

Blowing in the Wind

Ask your students what might happen if every plant simply dropped its seeds to the ground below. Explain that so many seeds sprouting in one place would mean many plants would be crowded out. How can the seeds spread out? The answer is blowing in the wind! Try this art activity to demonstrate how some seeds travel on the wind.

Give each child in a small group a sheet of blue construction paper, and ask her to draw a picture of either a fluffy white dandelion or a colorful flower. Then invite each child, in turn, to place her drawing inside a large foil pan. Have her sprinkle a bit of white glitter onto her dandelion or black glitter onto the center of her colored flower. Then have her gently blow on her drawing and observe what happens to the glitter seeds. Do they travel easily? Where do they land? What might happen if a strong wind, rather than a gentle breeze, blew across the flower? Continue until each child has had a turn to send some glittery seeds gliding.

Pop! Go the Seed Pods

The seeds of some plants—such as poppies and orchids—are so tiny, the wind simply picks them up and carries them along. Other plants give their seeds a push. The touch-me-not, a plant that grows in damp woodsy areas, is one of them. If you touch one when its seeds are fully ripe, its seed pods explode, scattering seeds into the air! Introduce your little ones to this interesting plant by showing them a picture of it from an encyclopedia or garden manual. Then give each child a handful of paper confetti seeds and invite him to act out this tune. You'll want to have a broom or vacuum handy afterward, but the fun will be worth the cleanup!

(sung to the tune of "Pop! Goes the Weasel")

There is a plant, the touch-me-not,

With seeds inside its seed pods.
The seeds, they grow and grow and grow...
Pop! Go the seed pods!

(Touch finger to hand holding confetti; then shake finger "no.")
(Point to confetti in cupped hand.)
(Wiggle hand holding confetti.)
(Open hand suddenly, tossing confettti into air.)

Water Travelers

Can seeds float? Set up this unusual float-and-sink center and invite your students to find out. Stock the center with a plastic tub filled with water, some of the seeds your students gathered during "Hitchhiking Seeds" (on page 13), plus maple seeds, acorns, dried beans and peas, assorted nuts in their shells, and a fresh coconut. Use a permanent marker to label one plastic disposable plate "Floaters" and another "Sinkers." Encourage youngsters at this center to test the various seeds and sort them onto the two plates. After everyone has had a turn to visit this center, invite youngsters to discuss their findings. Why would some seeds float? Share the information in "This Is Why" to enlighten your young scientists.

Floaters   Sinkers

This Is Why

Some plants can use water to help spread their seeds. Rainstorms, streams, rivers, and oceans carry seeds to new locations and help them spread out. Seeds that float, such as the coconut, have air-filled chambers inside them that make them float.

Where Are the Acorns?

Sometimes seeds travel with a little help from our animal friends, as youngsters will discover with this fun activity. In advance, make several copies of the acorn patterns on page 18 on brown construction paper. Cut out and laminate the acorns. Next, draw a simple tree on a large sheet of butcher paper. Ask student volunteers to color the tree; then mount it on a bulletin board. Use pushpins to mount the acorn patterns on the ground below the tree.

Explain to your students that animals help scatter seeds. Birds eat fruit and drop the seeds. Squirrels and other animals store seeds, such as acorns, by burying or hiding them. Sometimes the squirrels dig up the acorns; sometimes the acorns are left long enough that they sprout and begin to grow. When your group is out of the room, take the acorns off the display and hide them throughout your classroom. Challenge your youngsters to play the part of hungry squirrels and find them. When the hunt is over, see how many acorns were left behind to sprout and grow. Repeat the activity a few times, hiding the acorns in new places. Then teach little ones this song to help them remember how squirrels help seeds travel.

(sung to the tune of "My Bonnie Lies Over the Ocean")

A squirrel once found a small acorn.
He buried it deep in the ground.
He left and forgot it completely.
It sprouted and grew upward bound.
Hide seeds, hide seeds,
Oh, squirrels hide seeds in the ground, the ground!
Hide seeds, hide seeds,
Oh, squirrels hide seeds in the ground.

Just Rollin' Along

Acorns and other nuts aren't totally dependent on animals to scatter them. Find out another way nuts travel as your seed study goes rolling along! To prepare, purchase a small supply of pecans and walnuts in their shells. If acorns are plentiful in your area, ask students to help you collect some. Explain to your youngsters that many nuts—such as the ones you've collected for this activity—are the seeds of trees. Can they guess how nuts scatter? Try these experiments to find out.

First, ask a student volunteer to hold an acorn in the palm of his hand; then have him *gently* blow on the acorn. Does it move? Repeat the experiment with a pecan and then a walnut. Lead students to determine that nuts are too heavy to travel efficiently by air.

Next, ask three more volunteers to try to get the three types of nuts to stick to their socks. Can the nuts hitchhike? Point out that nuts do not have barbs or hooks to help them catch a ride on clothing or animal fur.

Finally, ask three more students to stand in front of the group and pretend to be trees. Direct them to hold their hands high above their heads to represent tree branches. Place one nut in each child's hand; then have him drop it. What happens? The nuts *roll away* from the tree! Invite more students to take on the role of a tree and check out the roll of the nut!

Seeds Travel Everywhere

Summarize some of the ways seeds travel by singing this song to the tune of "You Are My Sunshine."

Oh, seeds can travel
To many places.
They like to hitchhike
Or go by air.
Animals move some.
Some float on water.
Seeds can travel
To most anywhere!

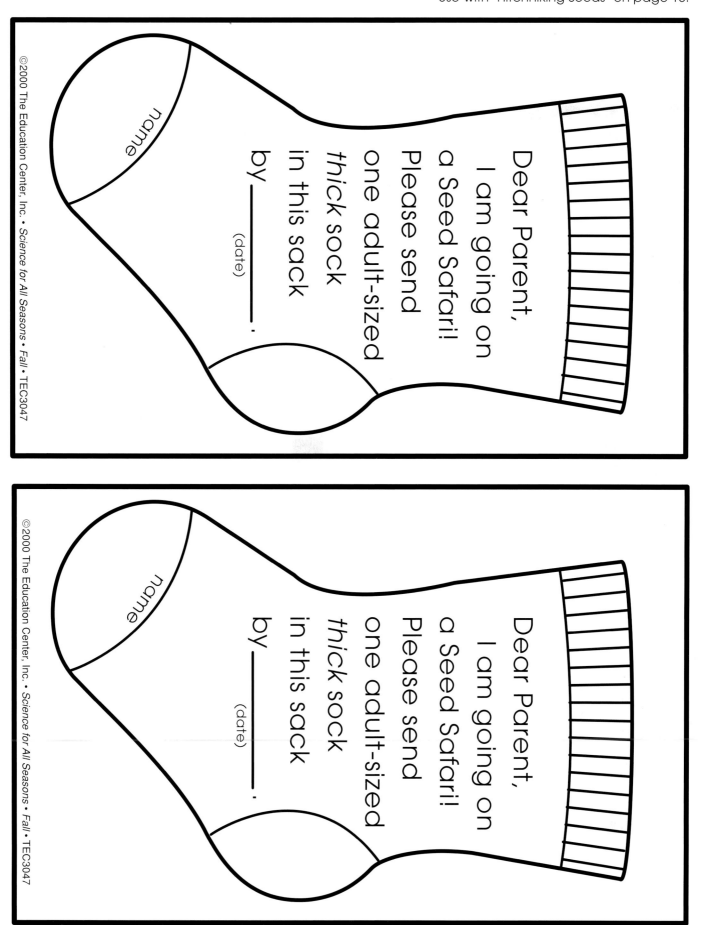

Dear Parent,
I am going on
a Seed Safari!
Please send
one adult-sized
thick sock
in this sack
by _____
(date)
.

name

Dear Parent,
I am going on
a Seed Safari!
Please send
one adult-sized
thick sock
in this sack
by _____
(date)
.

name

Acorn Patterns

Use with "Where Are the Acorns?" on page 15.

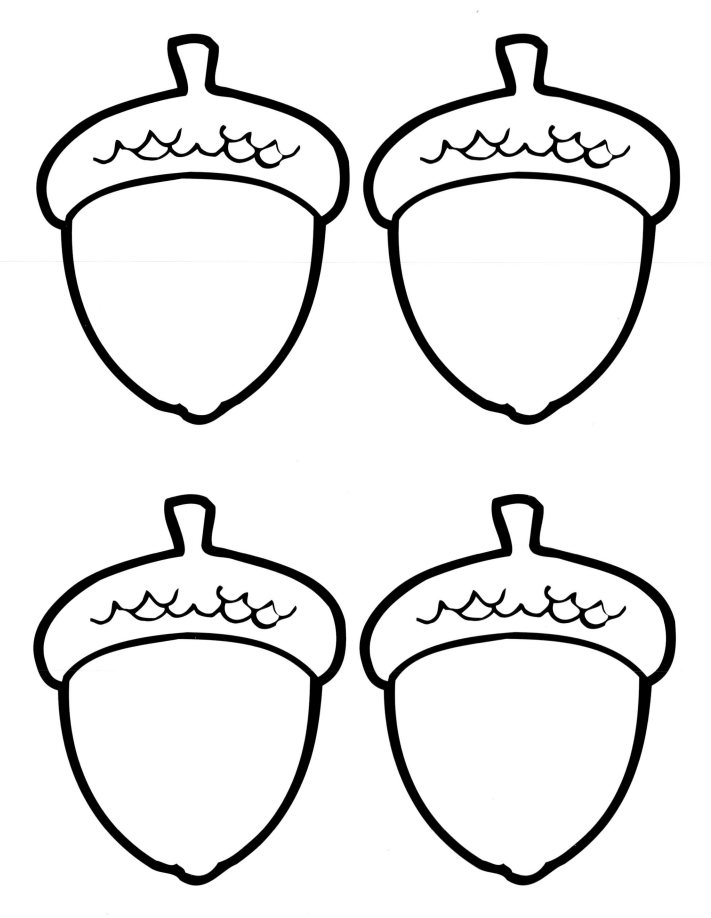

Eating Seeds

Seeds? To eat? Of course! Introduce your little ones to some yummy edible seeds with these savory scientific activities!

To Eat or Not to Eat?

Start your study of edible seeds with this simple sorting activity. In advance, gather a variety of seeds, such as popcorn (popped and unpopped), walnuts, acorns, lima beans (dried and canned), various flower seeds in packets, roasted pumpkin seeds, roasted peanuts, apple seeds, orange seeds, and a coconut. Identify each type of seed for your youngsters. Then teach them the following song:

(sung to the tune of "Do You Know the Muffin Man?")

Which seeds are the kind we eat,
Kind we eat, kind we eat?
Which seeds are the kind we eat?
Which ones will you choose?

Have your students help you sort the seeds into two baskets, labeled "Eat" and "Don't Eat." Discuss the results of your sorting; then remind students that although you'll be focusing on seeds that are edible, *not all seeds can be eaten.* Leave the various seeds and the baskets in a center for students to sort again independently. Then finish up this activity by serving students a popular seed snack: popcorn!

Eat

Don't Eat

Eating Seeds? Yes, Indeed!

Create this multidimensional display to help youngsters explore the variety of seeds that people eat. Near a bulletin board, set up a small table, and display cans of peas, beans, corn, and nuts, along with bags of popcorn, dried beans, rice, and cereals. Then invite your little investigators to get in on the act! Encourage your students to find and cut out pictures of edible seeds from magazines to mount on the bulletin board. Also ask students to bring in labels from canned, frozen, and packaged goods containing edible seeds. Add those to the display, as well as the plates created in "What's for Lunch?" on page 20. Title this delicious display "Eating Seeds? Yes, Indeed!"

19

What's for Lunch?

What's for lunch? Seeds! Invite your youngsters to serve up some seed-packed plates in this art activity. To prepare, set up serving stations, each with bottles of glue and a supply of one type of edible seed (see the list below for some choices). Clearly label each type of seed. Then give each child a paper plate divided into three sections. Have him choose three types of seeds to glue onto his plate; then help him copy the name of each seed on his plate. Add the finished plates to the display created in "Eating Seeds? Yes, Indeed!" on page 19. Want to *really* serve seeds for lunch? Invite youngsters to help you whip up the Seed Salad recipe on this page. Mmm!

Good Seeds for Gluing
- dried beans
- dried peas
- rice
- peanuts in the shell
- dry oatmeal
- sunflower seeds

Seed Salad
(makes 24 quarter-cup servings)

1 can (15 oz.) kidney beans
1 can (15 oz.) lima beans
1 can (15 oz.) whole kernel corn
1 can (15 oz.) French-style green beans
1 tbsp. sugar
1 bottle (8 oz.) Italian salad dressing

Drain the beans and corn; then combine them in a large bowl. Mix the dressing and sugar together; then pour it over the bean/corn mixture and toss. Refrigerate overnight.

Home Learning Lab

Invite little ones to share their knowledge of edible seeds with their families when they complete this activity at home. Duplicate page 22 and fill in the date desired. Then make a class supply of the programmed sheet. Have each child write her name on her sheet and take it home. When everyone has returned her sheet to class, help your little ones analyze the information gathered.

Edible Seeds at	Breyanna (name)	's House
peas		
peanuts		
popcorn		
walnuts		
green beans		
corn		
kidney beans		
sesame seeds		
coconut		
sunflower seeds		

Sampling Seeds

Your students and their preferences are the main ingredients for this tasty activity. In advance, purchase a bag of roasted pumpkin seeds and a bag of roasted sunflower seeds. Empty the two bags into separate bowls. Glue the empty bags to the top of a two-column graph (as shown). Then cut out a class set of construction paper seed shapes. Invite each child to taste both types of seeds and decide which she likes best. Have her write her name on a seed cutout and then place the cutout in the appropriate column on the graph. Discuss the results. Do your students prefer pumpkin, or are they stuck on sunflower?

A Nutty Surprise

Give your seed specialists an up-close peek at the world's largest known edible seed: the coconut. Place a fresh coconut inside a pillowcase. Tie a ribbon around the loose end of the case. Then pass the pillowcase around during your circle time. Encourage little ones to feel the mystery object and to take note of its weight and shape. Ask your students to brainstorm what might be inside the pillowcase. Jot their responses on your chalkboard. Next, untie the ribbon and invite each child to slip her hand into the case and feel the object *without peeking.* Ask again what the mystery object might be. When everyone has had a chance to guess, have your group count to three; then reveal the coconut! Pass the coconut around again and invite children to shake it. Then share some factual information about coconuts (see "Did You Know?"). Culminate this activity by cracking open the coconut and inviting each child to sample the juice and the meat. (If you don't wish to crack open the fresh coconut, have youngsters sample commercially packaged shredded coconut and coconut milk.)

Did You Know?

- The coconut is the world's largest known seed.
- The liquid inside is thin, clear coconut juice. It can be served as a fresh drink.
- The meat inside the coconut is white. It can be eaten raw or cooked.
- An average harvest of a coconut palm yields 60 coconuts. Some trees produce three times that many!

Match the Shell

If your students are nuts about edible seeds by now, try this inference activity that's perfect for small groups. To prepare, gather a supply of walnuts, pecans, almonds, and peanuts, both with shells and without. (Have enough nuts without shells on hand for each youngster to taste at the end of the activity, but be sure to check for nut allergies first.) Give each child one of each type of nut (with shells) to examine. Show youngsters a peanut without a shell, pointing out its size and shape. Ask youngsters to look at the sizes and shapes of their nuts with shells and to determine which one corresponds to the peanut without its shell. Repeat the process with the remaining nuts. Once youngsters have matched all the nuts with and without shells, provide nuts for them to taste. Who knew science could be so nutty?

Dear Parent,

What do peas, peanuts, and popcorn have in common? They're all seeds! Help your child discover what edible seeds you have at home with this checklist. Have your child check or color the box next to each type of seed he or she finds in your kitchen. Return the checklist to school by

_____.
(date)

Thanks for your help!

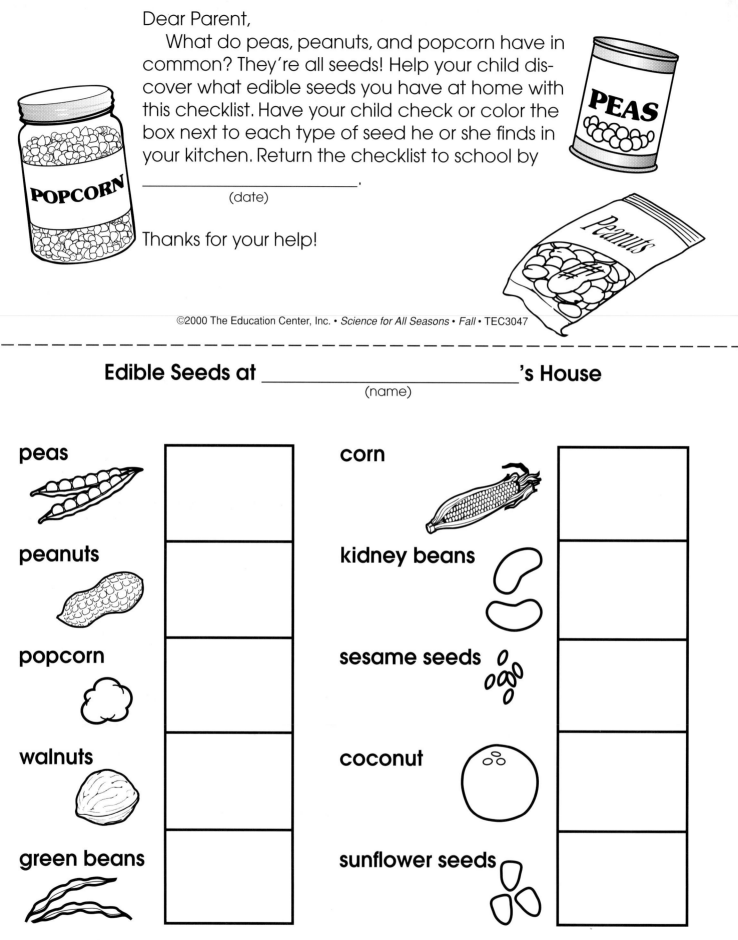

Edible Seeds at _____**'s House**
(name)

peas		corn	
peanuts		kidney beans	
popcorn		sesame seeds	
walnuts		coconut	
green beans		sunflower seeds	

Note to the teacher: Use with "Home Learning Lab" on page 20.

Rocks Rule!

Bumpy, shiny, smooth, or tiny—rocks make for some interesting explorations! Treat youngsters to these rockin' activities and they're sure to agree: when it comes to science, rocks rule!

Rocks

marble
— It is smooth.
— It has lines in it.

pumice stone
— It is white.
— It has little holes in it.
— It looks like a sponge, but it is hard.

Rocks at the Ready

To provide lots of hands-on learning opportunities for your little rock hounds, you'll need to gather a collection of rocks. Search your playground or your yard at home to find some common rocks in different sizes. Then visit a nature store, a craft store, or a garden center to purchase a wide variety of interesting rock specimens, such as those listed below.

To introduce your little ones to each special rock specimen, list its name on a chart. Ask youngsters to describe the rock as they pass it around. Write their descriptions on the chart. Then tell them a bit about how the rock was formed, and discuss where it might be found. Add the factual information to the chart and post it in your classroom during your rock study.

- **chalk**—made from the skeletons of tiny sea creatures
- **marble**—formed when limestone (another type of rock) is exposed to very hot temperatures
- **pumice stone**—formed from the cooled lava of a volcano. Gas bubbles in the lava create the holes in the stone.
- **rock salt**—comes from seawater or saltwater lakes and lagoons
- **concrete and brick**—man-made stones used in construction
- **pebbles**—can be formed when pieces of a cliff are broken up by the waves of the sea
- **rock crystal**—a type of mineral called quartz. Quartz is used in some watches to help keep time.

For more information and photos of many types of rocks, check out a nonfiction book about rocks from your library, such as *Rocks and Minerals* (Eyewitness Books) by R. F. Symes (Dorling Kindersley).

Sing a Rock Song

Where do your rock hounds like to hunt for rocks? In the sandbox or deep in the dirt? In a favorite pond or along the road? Teach your youngsters this song to reinforce the idea that rocks are found in many places in our environment. Review your rock specimen chart to help students recall places where rocks can be found. To create new verses, use student suggestions for different locations to substitute in the third line of the song.

(sung to the tune of "Oh Where, Oh Where Has My Little Dog Gone?")

Oh where, oh where can we find some rocks?
Oh where, oh where can rocks be?
We can find some special rocks [in the sand]
If we just look and see!

Gee, We're Geologists!

One place your students are *sure* to find rocks is this rock exploration site at your sand table! Invite your students to play the part of geologists at this center set up for finding, identifying, and examining rocks. Provide children's hard hats, safety goggles, gloves, magnifying glasses, sand sieves, and clean paintbrushes at the center. Bury your rock specimens (gathered for "Rocks at the Ready" on page 23) in the sand. Photocopy pictures of the rocks from an encyclopedia or rock guide. Post the pictures near your sand table. Encourage your pint-sized geologists to unearth the rocks and then compare each one to the posted pictures to identify it.

Deanne's Rock Report

This is rock crystal. It's shiny and pink.

Rock Reports

Since all good scientists document their findings, set up an area where your junior geologists can report on their rock explorations at your sand table. Provide students with rock-shaped paper, pencils, and crayons at a table near your sand area. After a student identifies some rock specimens from the sand table, have her take them to this documentation area. Ask her to draw a picture of each rock on a separate sheet of paper. Write her dictation as she describes each rock and how she identified it. Then staple the papers together behind an additional rock-shaped page to form a booklet. Title each child's booklet "[Child's name]'s Rock Report."

Rock Talk

If your little ones are eager to dig up more about rocks, read aloud *On My Beach There Are Many Pebbles* by Leo Lionni (Mulberry Books). This book will provide students with a close-up and creative look at rocks. During a second reading, ask students to identify the types of pebbles described by the author, such as strange, wonderful, letterpebbles, and peoplepebbles. List the words on a sheet of chart paper. Later, use the chart as a reference as students examine some of the rocks from your class collection. Hold up one rock and have a student give an adjective or descriptive name similar to those in the story. Review the words on your chart to help students with their descriptions. Repeat this process a few times. Then ask each child to choose a rock from your collection to hold. Have each child, in turn, give an adjective or descriptive name for his rock. Then ask each youngster to save his rock for use in the booklet activity that follows.

ordinary
wonderful
fishpebbles
numberpebbles
peoplepebbles

eggrock!

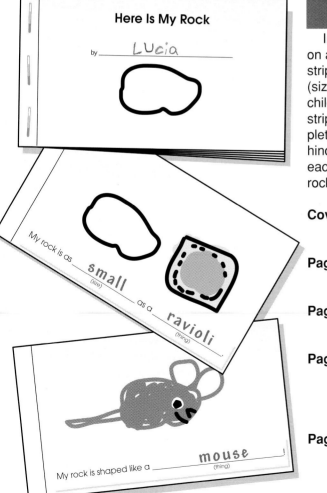

Here Is My Rock

Invite each of your students to create a descriptive booklet focusing on a favorite rock. To prepare, duplicate the booklet cover and text strips on page 28 to make a class supply. For each child, cut four pages (sized to match the booklet cover) from white copy paper. Have each child cut out her booklet cover and text strips. Have her glue one text strip to the bottom of each of her four pages. Direct each child to complete her pages as described. Then help her sequence her pages behind the cover and staple the booklet together along the left side. Place each child's completed booklet in a zippered plastic bag along with her rock; then have her take the project home to share with her family.

Cover: Write your name on the line. Lay your rock on the cover and trace around it with a pencil. Then go over your pencil outline with a black marker.

Page 1: Lay your rock on the page and trace around it with a pencil. Next to the outline, draw a picture of an object that is the same size as your rock. Fill in the blanks in the text.

Page 2: Lay your rock on the page and trace around it with a pencil. Color in the outline with a crayon that matches the color of your rock. Fill in the blanks in the text.

Page 3: Lay your rock on the page and trace around it with a pencil. Put a small square of white tissue paper on top of your real rock. Gently color on the tissue with a crayon to create a rubbing. Glue the rubbing to the rock outline on the page. Fill in the blanks in the text.

Page 4: Lay your rock on the page and trace around it with a pencil. Use crayons and/or your pencil to make your rock outline resemble an object or animal. Fill in the blank in the text.

Opposite Rocks

Ask youngsters to further explore rocks' sizes, textures, and colors with this comparison activity. To prepare, sort through your classroom rock collection to find a few big rocks, small rocks, light-colored rocks, dark-colored rocks, rough rocks, and smooth rocks. To begin the activity, lay the rocks on a table and invite a small group of students to join you there. Ask a student volunteer to find a big rock and its opposite, a little rock. Ask another child to find a different pair of big and little rocks. Next, ask other students to find light- and dark-colored pairs and rough and smooth pairs. Continue until every child has had plenty of opportunities to compare a variety of rocks that have contrasting attributes.

Rock Attribute Song

Big and small, light and dark, rough and smooth…your rock lovers have found that rocks have lots of interesting attributes! Reinforce this descriptive vocabulary when you teach youngsters this song.

(sung to the tune of "The Mulberry Bush")

We know that rocks can be [big or small],
[Big or small], [big or small].
We know that rocks can be [big or small],
Rocks come in different [sizes].

Repeat the verse two more times, substituting the attributes below for the underlined words.
light or dark…colors
rough or smooth…textures

Rock Sorting Center

Since rocks have so many attributes, they're perfect for sorting! To prepare a sorting center, fill a container with a variety of rocks and set out several large paper plates and some plastic magnifying glasses. Ask students at this center to sort the stones into groups by attributes: size, shape, color, texture, or any other attribute they choose! Have them place each group of rocks on a separate paper plate. Check in at this center periodically and ask students to describe the attributes they used to sort the rocks.

Home Learning Lab

Encourage parents to dig in to your rock topic as they assist their little ones in a rock hunt. Duplicate the parent note on page 29 to make a class supply. Place each child's copy of the note in a zippered plastic bag and have her take it home. When she returns the checklist to school, discuss the different types of rocks she found on her rock hunt. Invite her to show her classmates the rock she brought from home and to describe its color, size, and texture.

Let's Go on a Rock Hunt!

Dear Parent,
We are studying rocks at school! Read the list below; then take your child on a rock hunt around your home. How many of these rocks can you find? Make a check mark beside each rock you and your child find. Then choose one of the rocks to send to school in this plastic bag. Have your child bring his or her checklist and rock to school on ___October 9___ . After your child shows his or
(date)
her rock to the class, it will be returned. Thank you for supporting your child's learning!

___ chalk
___ marble
___ pumice stone
___ rock crystal
✔ brick
___ rock salt
✔ concrete
✔ gravel
✔ pebbles

Which can has rocks?

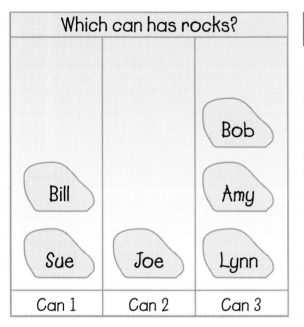

Bill		Bob
Sue	Joe	Amy
		Lynn
Can 1	Can 2	Can 3

There's a Whole Lotta Shakin' Goin' On!

Inquiring minds want to know—which can is full of rocks? That's the question in this fun inference activity. To prepare, cover three Pringles® potato chip cans and lids with construction paper. Put some small rocks into one can, some pennies into another, and some popped popcorn into the third; then place the lids on all three cans. Label each can with a different number: 1, 2, or 3. Next, prepare a three-column graph as shown. Then cut a class supply of small rock shapes from gray construction paper.

To begin, show your group the three cans and explain that one of the three contains rocks. Explain that you're going to shake each can as they listen carefully. After you've shaken all three cans, give each child a rock cutout and ask her to write her name on it. Ask her to place her rock on the graph to represent her guess. Have a few student volunteers explain their reasoning. Then open all the cans and reveal the contents of each one. Did students' inquiry skills help them guess correctly? Repeat the activity on another day, if desired, substituting different materials for the pennies and popcorn.

Independent Inquiry Center

Invite your young scientists to create their own Inquiry Cans in this noisemaking, can-shaking center! To prepare, cover several snack-sized Pringles® potato chip cans and lids with construction paper. Also provide margarine tubs filled with pebbles, cotton balls, coins, dried pasta, dried beans, paper clips, and any other noisy (or not-so-noisy) items you have available. At this center, a child places pebbles in one potato chip can and fills the other cans with the materials of his choice. He then finds a friend to join him at the center. The partner shakes the cans and guesses which can holds the pebbles. It's true—two scientists have more fun than one!

Booklet Cover

Use with "Here Is My Rock" on page 25.

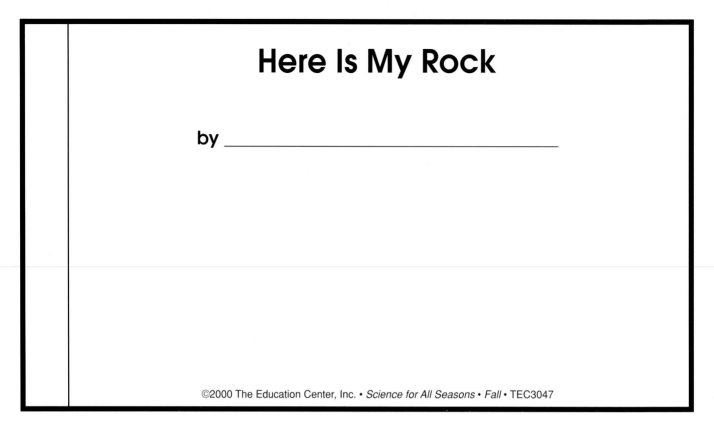

Here Is My Rock

by _____

Text Strips

Use with "Here Is My Rock" on page 25.

My rock is as _____ as a _____ .
(size)   (thing)

My rock is as _____ as a _____ .
(color)   (thing)

My rock is as _____ as a _____ .
(texture)   (thing)

My rock is shaped like a _____ !
(thing)

Let's Go on a Rock Hunt!

Dear Parent,

    We are studying rocks at school! Read the list below; then take your child on a rock hunt around your home. How many of these rocks can you find? Make a check mark beside each rock you and your child find. Then choose one of the rocks to send to school in this plastic bag. Have your child bring his or her checklist and rock to school on _____. After your child shows his or her rock to the class, it will be returned. Thank you for supporting your child's learning!

                    (date)

_____ chalk

_____ marble

_____ pumice stone

_____ rock crystal

_____ brick

_____ rock salt

_____ concrete

_____ gravel

_____ pebbles

Note to the teacher: Use with "Home Learning Lab" on page 27.

Buildings Galore

Open the door to learning excitement with this unit exploring the science and art of buildings. Your budding architects are sure to blossom!

Huff and Puff

Huff and puff your way into the science of building by reading your favorite version of *The Three Little Pigs.* Then sing the song below. After each verse, discuss with students what happened to that particular house in the story.

(sung to the tune of "Did You Ever See a Lassie?")

Have you ever seen a pig's house,
A pig's house, a pig's house?
Have you ever seen a pig's house,
A house made of [straw]?
When you huff and you puff,
Does that house stay real tough?
Have you ever seen a pig's house,
A house made of [straw]?

Repeat, substituting the underlined word with sticks *and then* bricks *in turn.*

Building Time!

Now it's time for your little architects to test their own building abilities by crafting each of the three pigs' homes. To prepare, set up a house-building center with the following items: straw, hay, or raffia; craft sticks or twigs; and LEGO® bricks or blocks. Place a copy of *The Three Little Pigs* in the center so youngsters can refer to the pigs' building techniques. Invite each child to visit the center and construct a straw house, a stick house, and a brick house. When he has completed each house, encourage him to check its sturdiness by huffing and puffing and trying to blow his *own* house down! After each child has had an opportunity to visit the center, discuss which materials were the sturdiest and which were the easiest to use.

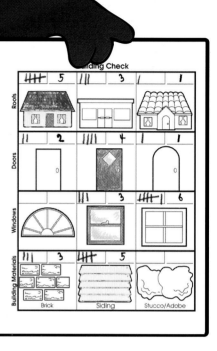

Building Check

Now that your little ones are focused on building materials, it's time to check out real buildings in your school's neighborhood. Before taking a stroll, make a copy of page 35 for each child; then staple each sheet to a piece of sturdy cardboard. Supply each child with a crayon and a copy of page 35. Discuss the pictures on page 35 with your students; then head outside! (If you are unable to take your students on a neighborhood walk, have youngsters look through real estate magazines.) Encourage each child to examine different buildings for the items on her sheet. When a child spies one of the items, have her make a tally mark in the appropriate box. After returning to your classroom, have each child add up the marks in each box and then write the number on the corresponding line. Discuss which items were seen the most; then direct each child to color those items on her sheet. Happy house hunting!

This Is Why

Roofs are shaped differently for various kinds of weather. Slanted roofs are needed to let rain run off; flat roofs are fine in hot, dry areas with little rain.

A Weatherproof Roof

Weather has a lot to do with the way a building's roof is constructed. Use this activity to help your students understand why some roofs are flat and some are slanted by experimenting with milk carton houses. Gather the materials listed; then have each child follow the steps below to complete the activity.

Materials needed for each child:
1 clean cardboard milk carton with the top cut off
1 paper towel
1 eyedropper
two 5" x 7" index cards
access to a container of water

Steps:
1. Place a milk carton on a paper towel.
2. Place an index card on top of the carton to create a flat roof.
3. Fill the eyedropper with water, and then use it to make raindrops on the roof. Observe the drops to see if they roll easily off the roof.
4. Remove the flat roof. Make a slanted roof by folding the other index card in half and then placing it on the carton.
5. Repeat Step 3 to see if the drops behave differently.

Brick Walls

Looking at a brick wall firsthand will certainly reinforce this wall-building activity. (If you don't have a brick building nearby, show youngsters pictures from magazines or encyclopedias.) Have the children look for the brick pattern in the wall and observe the material between the bricks. Explain that the material between the bricks is *mortar,* a mixture that holds the bricks together.

After examining and observing brick walls with your students, have each child build her own edible wall. To begin, provide each child with the following: 1 paper towel, 6 large marshmallows (bricks), 1 plastic knife, and 1 tbsp. peanut butter (mortar). Direct each child to align her marshmallows into layers as shown, and then have her try gently toppling the marshmallows. Next, have each child use the peanut butter mortar to stick her marshmallow bricks together. Then challenge her to try toppling the wall again. Lead your little ones to conclude that the peanut butter mortar helps make the wall more sturdy. Now invite your young bricklayers to devour their tasty creations!

Little Levels

While constructing a building, all builders use a device called a *level* to make sure the building foundations are horizontal. Use this activity and have each child make and use her own level. In advance, collect a class supply of transparent 35mm film canisters with lids. Use a ruler and a permanent marker to make a straight line on each canister from the top to the bottom. Have each child fill his canister halfway with tinted water and then place the lid on the canister.

To use the level, direct each child to place it on a surface and observe the water in the canister. If the water lines up evenly with the line on the canister, the surface is level. If the water and the line do not line up, then the surface is not level. Encourage the child to use her level to test various surfaces in the classroom; then discuss student findings with the class.

Building Search

Houses are just one kind of building found in a community. Encourage youngsters to create a building collage by cutting out pictures of various structures from magazines and realty catalogs. Then instruct the children to glue the pictures to a large sheet of bulletin board paper. Next, have the children sing this song about buildings:

(sung to the tune of "Ten Little Indians")

Houses, churches, office buildings,
Shopping malls, apartment dwellings,
Hotels, motels, tall skyscrapers,
All of these are buildings.

Home Learning Lab

Don't lock parents out of learning fun! Invite them to participate with this take-home activity that has youngsters observing and comparing roofs around their neighborhoods! Duplicate page 36 for each child to take home, complete, and then return. On the designated day, graph the results; then discuss them.

A Building Looks Like This

Now that youngsters are familiar with buildings, invite each child to create a building booklet to share with his family. To make one booklet, duplicate pages 37–39 onto construction paper. Cut apart the booklet pages. Stack the pages in order; then staple them along the left side. Read through the directions below and gather the necessary materials. Then have each student follow the directions below to complete each page. When each child has completed a booklet, have him share it with the class.

Cover: Write your name; then color the pictures.
Page 1: Cut out and glue on a construction paper roof; then color the picture.
Page 2: Sponge-paint red bricks.
Page 3: Cut out magazine pictures of windows; then glue them onto the page.
Page 4: Cut out magazine pictures of doors; then glue them onto the page.
Page 5: Draw a building. Cut out a construction paper door; then fold it back as shown. Glue the door to the page along the folded edge. Draw a picture of yourself in the doorway.

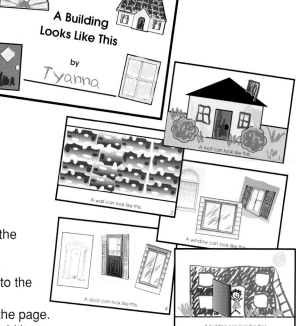

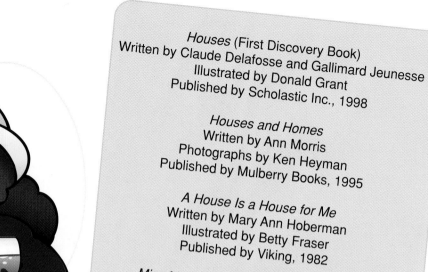

Houses (First Discovery Book)
Written by Claude Delafosse and Gallimard Jeunesse
Illustrated by Donald Grant
Published by Scholastic Inc., 1998

Houses and Homes
Written by Ann Morris
Photographs by Ken Heyman
Published by Mulberry Books, 1995

A House Is a House for Me
Written by Mary Ann Hoberman
Illustrated by Betty Fraser
Published by Viking, 1982

Miss Malarkey Doesn't Live in Room 10
Written by Judy Finchler
Illustrated by Kevin O'Malley
Published by Walker Publishing Company, Inc.; 1995

How a House Is Built
Written and Illustrated by Gail Gibbons
Published by Holiday House, Inc.; 1996

Centered on Building

Extend the theme of construction throughout your classroom with these learning center ideas.

Block Center: Invite students to visit the block center to build walls. Encourage the youngsters to use different patterns when building the walls; then test each structure for stability by gently bumping the wall.

Sand Table: Stock your sand table with a supply of LEGO® blocks and several building levels (See "Little Levels" on page 32). Remind your little builders how the level works; then challenge the children to build a level LEGO house.

Math Center: Encourage students to build tall towers from Lincoln Logs®, cardboard bricks, wooden blocks, or colorful sponges. Have each student construct a tower until it topples. Post a chart nearby for youngsters to record the number of blocks that were used before their towers collapsed.

Art Center: Stock this center with rectangular sponges, pans of red paint, glue, and white construction paper. Direct each child to use a sponge and paint to print a brick pattern on a sheet of construction paper. When the paint is dry, invite the child to add construction paper windows, a door, and a roof.

Reading Center: Make a cozy reading shelter by covering three sides of a table with a sheet. Then stock the area with the books about houses and homes listed above.

Building Check

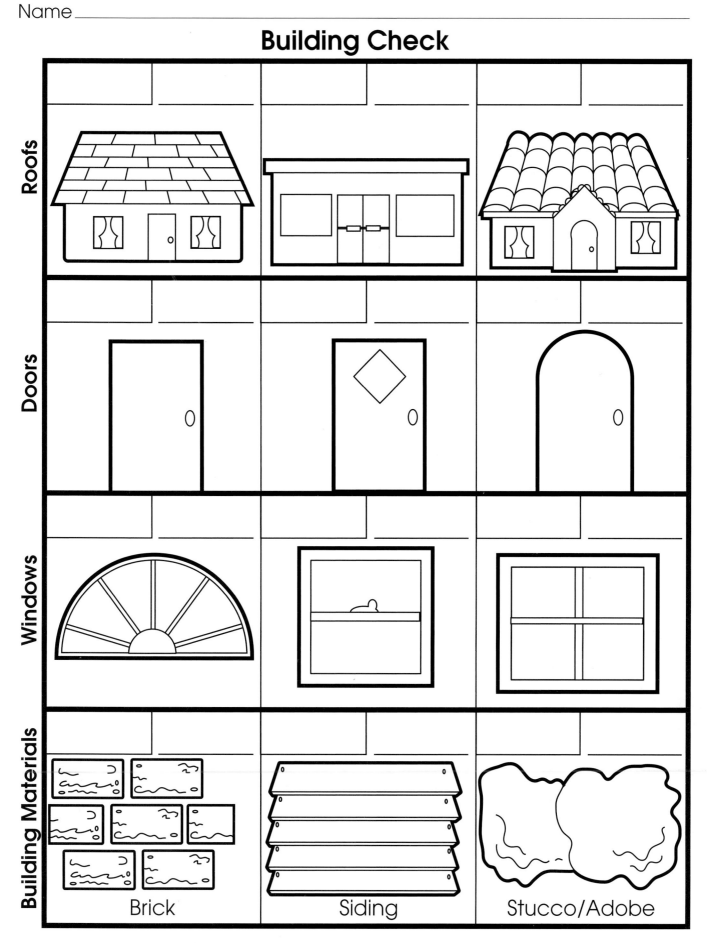

Roofs

Doors

Windows

Building Materials

Brick

Siding

Stucco/Adobe

Note to the teacher: Use with "Building Check" on page 31.

35

Roof Reporter

Dear Parent,

   Your child is learning about buildings and their features. Please help him or her continue exploration at home by completing this activity. Instruct your child to take a good look at the roof of your home and the surrounding buildings. Then have him or her draw a picture of your roof in the space below. Please send this completed sheet to school with your child by_____.

(date)

A Building Looks Like This

by

_____

©2000 The Education Center, Inc. • *Science for All Seasons* • *Fall* • TEC3047

A roof can look like this.

1

A wall can look like this.   2

A window can look like this.   3

A door can look like this.

4

A building can look like this!

5

Science Book Spectrum

Fall Features

Fall into autumn with these colorful books full of seasonal sights.

When Autumn Comes

Written and Photo-illustrated by Robert Maass
Published by Owlet, 1992

Does your part of the world enjoy a distinct seasonal change in autumn? Even if your youngsters encounter only subtle fall changes, this book will give the children a chance to study the bright leaves, sparkling frosts, and plump pumpkins of a northern autumn! After reading the book, have students recall fall weather, activities, plants, and clothing. Write student responses on a pumpkin-shaped chart. Substitute the words on the chart in the third line to create more verses for the song below. When you have sung several verses of the song, ask each child to name her favorite thing about autumn.

(sung to the tune of "Daisy")

Autumn is a wonderful time of year.
I like autumn. I'm glad that autumn's here!
Oh, [pumpkins] are right in season,
And that's a special reason
That autumn's neat. It can't be beat!
It's a wonderful time of year!

Autumn is a wonderful time of year.
I like autumn. I'm glad that autumn's here!
Oh, [raking] is right in season,
And that's a special reason
That autumn's neat. It can't be beat!
It's a wonderful time of year!

pumpkins
raking
scarecrow
jackets
trick-or-treat
corn
leaves
apple cider

Raccoons and Ripe Corn

Written and Illustrated by Jim Arnosky
Published by Mulberry Books, 1991

The rowdy raccoons in this autumn tale enjoy a fall feast of tasty corn. Your little ones will harvest information with this Indian-corn observation activity. To complete the activity, gather the materials listed and have each child follow the steps below.

Materials needed for each child:
1 copy of page 43
1 ear of Indian corn (seven inches or less)
access to a supply of sticky dots
crayons
a piece of yarn
glue
access to a balance scale and counting blocks
scissors

Steps:
1. Lay the ear of corn in the large box on the record sheet. Use sticky dots as shown to record the length of the corn on the sheet.
2. Wrap a piece of yarn around the middle of the corn and then cut off the excess yarn. Glue the yarn on the record sheet as shown.
3. Weigh the ear of corn on a balance scale. Count the number of blocks it takes to balance the scale; then draw the same number of blocks in the small box on page 43.
4. Remove a kernel from the ear of corn, and then glue the kernel in the small circle.

The Pumpkin Patch

Written and Photo-illustrated by Elizabeth King
Published by Econo-Clad Books, 1999

This pumpkin-filled picture book is a wonderful introduction to studying the growth cycle of a plant from seed to fruit. After you've read the book, revisit and discuss the pages that illustrate the stages of pumpkin growth; then teach your youngsters this poem to reinforce pumpkin growth stages.

First you plant the pumpkin seeds;
Then water them with care.
Soon the leaves and vines grow out,
And reach from here to there.
Little yellow blossoms bloom.
Pumpkins begin to show.
And from little pumpkin seeds,
Big orange pumpkins grow!

Pumpkin Seed Investigation

For more pumpkin science fun, invite a small group of students to predict, estimate, and count the seeds inside a baking pumpkin. In advance, cover a table with paper for easy cleanup. Gather the materials listed; then follow the steps below. When each small group has completed a seed investigation, compare each group's results to get the real scoop on pumpkin seeds.

Materials needed for one small group:
1 baking pumpkin
1 carving knife *(for teacher use only)*
1 metal spoon
paper towels
1 orange paper plate
2 green construction paper leaf cutouts
one 2" x 3" green construction paper stem cutout
1 green pipe cleaner
access to a stapler
pencil

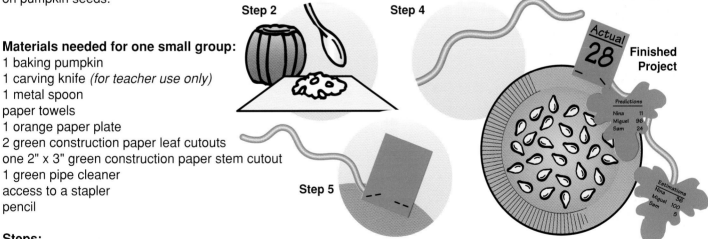

Steps:
1. Use the carving knife to cut off the top of the baking pumpkin; then remove one seed to show the group. Ask the students to *predict* how many seeds are inside the pumpkin. Record their responses on a leaf cutout; label it "Predictions."
2. Have each child, in turn, use the spoon to scoop out the pumpkin seeds and place them on a paper towel. Then invite youngsters to *estimate* the number of seeds. Record their responses on the second leaf cutout; label it "Estimations."
3. Have the students count the seeds; then direct one child to write the total number of seeds on the stem cutout. Label the stem "Actual."
4. Have a child bend the pipe cleaner to resemble a vine as shown.
5. Staple the stem and vine to the back edge of the paper plate as shown. Then staple the leaves onto the vine.
6. Instruct the students to glue their seeds in the center of the plate.
7. Encourage the group to discuss the results.

Red Leaf, Yellow Leaf

Written and Illustrated by Lois Ehlert
Published by Harcourt Brace Jovanovich, Publishers; 1991

Nothing symbolizes fall better than beautiful yellow, orange, and red autumn leaves. In this colorful picture book, Lois Ehlert's collage-style leaves seem ready to pop off the pages and blow away in the autumn breeze! As you read the book, give students plenty of time to study the pictures of the beautiful maple leaves.

Feel a Leaf

Use this inquiry activity to help your youngsters focus on the unique shapes of leaves. In advance, use the leaf patterns on page 44 to make tagboard tracers; then use the tracers to make a set of felt leaves. Arrange the felt leaves on a flannelboard; then place the tagboard leaves in your pocket. To begin the activity, secretly place one of the leaves from your pocket in a feelie bag. Invite a child to put her hand inside the bag, feel the leaf, and then find the matching leaf on the flannelboard. Encourage the child to explain why she thinks the two leaves match; then have her take the leaf out of the bag to see if she is correct. Continue the inquiry process until each child has had a turn.

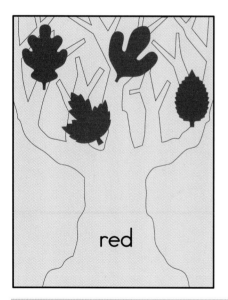

red

yellow

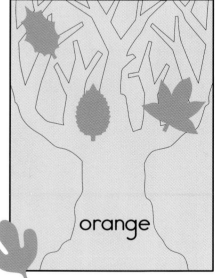

orange

Leaf Classification Center

Now it's time for your little leaf lookers to study the colors of fall foliage! In advance, make a red, a yellow, and an orange construction paper copy of the leaf patterns on page 44. Cut out the leaves; then place them in a basket. Next, make classification mats by making three copies of page 45 on tan construction paper. Label one mat "red," one mat "yellow," and one mat "orange." Place the mats and the basket of leaves at a center; then invite each child to use the mats to sort the leaves by color. To extend the classification opportunities, have each student sort the leaves by shape; then place the leaves on unprogrammed classification mats. Trees come alive with color!

Name _____

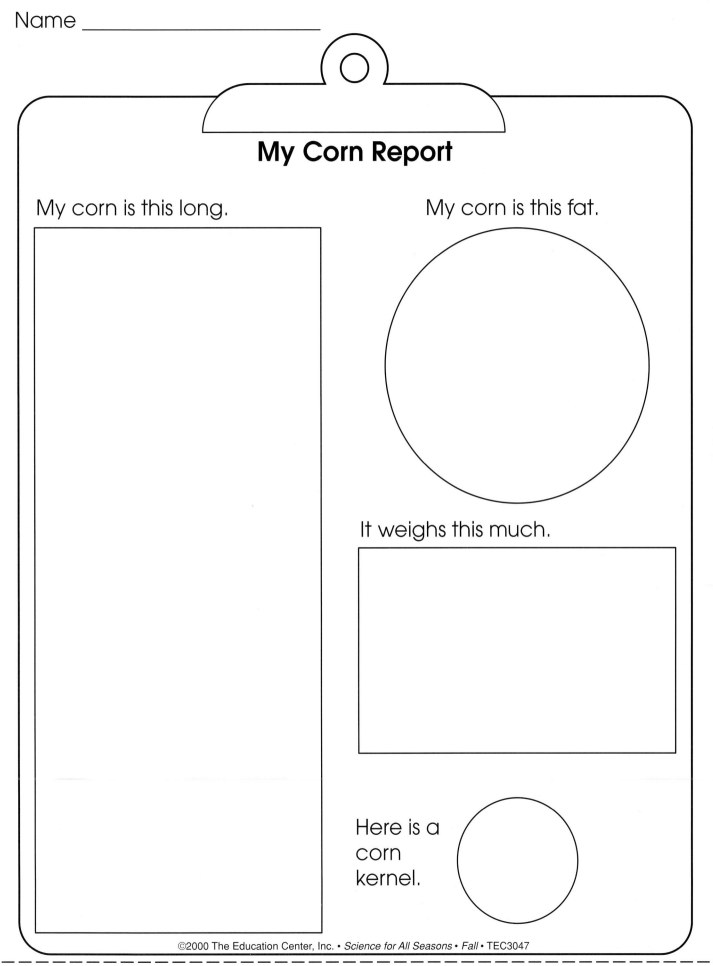

My Corn Report

My corn is this long.

My corn is this fat.

It weighs this much.

Here is a corn kernel.

Leaf Patterns

Use with "Feel a Leaf" and "Leaf Classification Center" on page 42.

The Scientific Artist

Digging Into Dough

Fortify fine-motor skills and thinking skills as your students knead, roll, and press through these doughy science explorations.

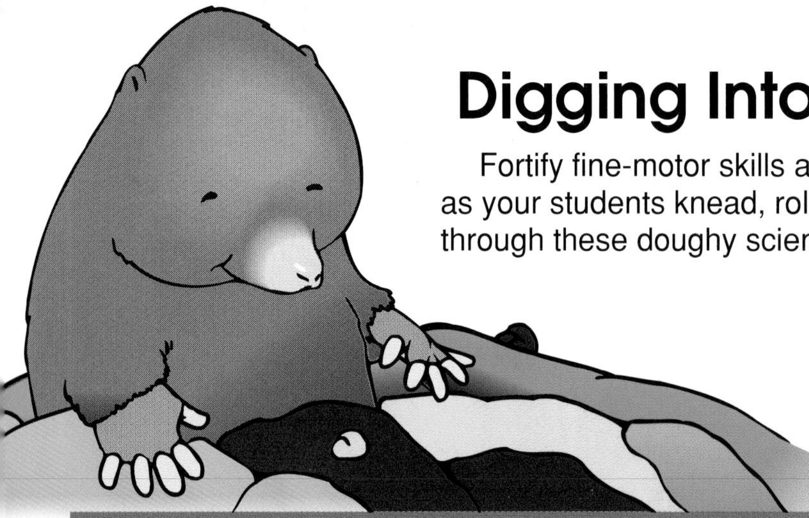

Dough Delight

Dive into your dough study with this hands-on investigation that also reinforces language skills. In advance, follow the recipe below to prepare a batch of play dough. Then give each child a small ball of dough to roll, squeeze, and sculpt. As your students explore with the dough, discuss with them how it feels, looks, and smells. Encourage students to describe different ways they handle the dough (roll, squish, pinch, etc.); then record their observations on chart paper. Save the chart and refer to it again in "D-O-U-G-H" below.

Delightful Dough
4 c. flour
1/2 c. iodized salt
1 3/4 c. warm water
a few drops of food coloring
Combine the flour and salt in a bowl; then stir in the warm water and food coloring. Knead the dough for ten minutes. Keep the dough refrigerated in an airtight container.

roll

squish

pinch

D-O-U-G-H

Teach your students this song using the action words from the chart created in "Dough Delight" above.

(sung to the tune of "Bingo")

What are some things we do with dough?
What can we do with play dough?
We can [roll] the dough!
We can [roll] the dough!
We can [roll] the dough!
It's fun to [roll] the play dough!

Dry Discovery

Mix inferential thinking skills with exploration as your students dig into the dough. To begin, invite a small group of students to observe as you mix together two cups of flour and one-half cup of iodized salt. Stir in teaspoons of warm water, one at a time, until the mixture begins to crumble. Then place a small amount of the mixture in a separate bowl for each child. Ask him to try to form a ball with his mixture. Then have him hypothesize why his mixture won't stick together. Lead him to conclude that the mixture needs more water. Next, provide the child with a small container of warm water and a teaspoon. Direct him to add water to his mixture, one teaspoon at a time, until the dough is sticky enough to form a ball. Allow each child some time to explore his dough; then have him place it in a personalized resealable plastic bag. Set the bags aside to use in "Air-Dried Dough" on page 48.

Detective Dough

Practice the scientific process skills of observing and inferring as your students investigate dough. Gather your students to observe as you mix two cups of flour, one-half cup of iodized salt, and $1\frac{3}{4}$ cups of warm water in a bowl. Stir the mixture and show students that it is too runny to form a ball. Lead students to conclude that adding more dry ingredients is necessary to make play dough. Gradually add two cups of flour and one-half cup of iodized salt to the mixture; then stir it to a doughy consistency. Refrigerate the dough in an airtight container to use in "Baked Dough" on page 48.

Just Dough It!

Teach your students this playful tune as you mix up a batch of play dough!

(sung to the tune of "Did You Ever See a Lassie?")

Have you ever made some play dough,
Some play dough, some play dough?
Have you ever made some play dough?
Let me tell you how!
You mix up some flour, some salt, and some water.
Have you ever made some play dough?
Let's make some right now!

Air-Dried Dough

Your students will begin thinking like scientists with this comparison activity. To begin, provide each child with the resealable plastic bag containing the dough from "Dry Discovery" (page 47). Have him divide the dough in half and then roll each half into a ball. Direct him to seal one ball inside his plastic bag. Then have the child place both balls on a personalized paper plate. Ask him to predict which dough ball will dry and harden first. Then place the plate on a table where it will be undisturbed. Encourage the child to check his experiment often to observe any changes. When the dough on the plate is hard and dry, have the child compare the texture and shape of the two balls. Then invite the child to hypothesize why the unbagged dough dried out. Save the dough in the plastic bag to use in "Home Learning Lab" (below).

This Is Why

The unbagged ball of dough was exposed to the air, which allowed the water in the dough to *evaporate*. The dough in the bag could not dry because the plastic blocked the water from evaporating into the air.

Baked Dough

Now that your students know that dough can be air-dried, try this experiment to show how heat also can change dough. In advance, collect two snack-sized resealable plastic bags for each child. Then duplicate page 52 to make a class supply. Roll out the dough from "Detective Dough" (page 47) to a quarter-inch thickness. Then have each child use a cookie cutter to cut two circles. Ask the child to put one circle in a resealable bag and staple it to the left side of the record sheet. Then help him complete the "Before" sentences. Next, have him use a toothpick to scratch his name into his second dough circle. Place all of the personalized circles on a cookie sheet and bake them at 300° until light brown. Remove the circles from the oven and let them cool. Then have each child put his baked dough into a resealable plastic bag. Staple the bag to the right side of the record sheet, and then help him complete the "After" sentences. Discuss with your students the differences in size, texture, and color of the two samples. Lead them to conclude that the heat of the oven caused the dough to change.

Name Tyra

Before the dough is baked it looks...
White, smooth, and flat.
it feels...
cool and soft.

Staple bag of unbaked dough here.

Baked Dough

After the dough is baked it looks...
bumpy and brownish.
it feels...
hard.

Staple bag of baked dough here.

Tyra

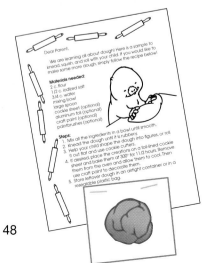

Home Learning Lab

Encourage parent and child interaction when each child takes home a salt dough recipe and a sample of the dough. To prepare, duplicate the parent note on page 51 for each child. Then staple the note to the plastic bag containing her dough from "Air-Dried Dough." Send home the note with the dough to encourage a "dough-lightful" home learning experience!

Dough Differences

Use this small-group activity to get your youngsters exploring different types of dough. To prepare, gather a batch of modeling clay and a batch of play dough. Then follow the recipe below to make a batch of peanut butter play dough. (Set aside a small portion of each type of dough to use in "Dough You Know?" below.) Place the three types of dough at a table; then post three sheets of chart paper near the table. Label one sheet "Clay," one sheet "Play Dough," and one sheet "Peanut Butter Play Dough." Invite a group of youngsters to the area and provide each child with a small sample of modeling clay. Have them explore and experiment with the clay; then invite them to describe it. Write their responses on the appropriate chart. Repeat the procedure with the play dough and again with the peanut butter play dough. After exploring all three doughs, invite students to make general observations about the differences in the doughs. If desired, record these responses on a chart labeled "Observations."

Clay
- It's hard
- It isn't easy to roll into a ball.

Peanut Butter Play Dough
- It smells good!
- It's kind of sticky.

Play Dough
- It stretches
- I can make a ball with it.

Peanut Butter Play Dough
1 c. peanut butter
1 c. honey or corn syrup
1 c. powdered milk
1 c. oatmeal
   Thoroughly mix all of the ingredients in a large bowl until a ball of dough forms.

Thumbs-Up!

This center activity is a great way for each child to communicate what she discovered in "Dough Differences" (above). In advance, make a copy of the recording sheet on page 53 for each child. Then place samples of clay, play dough, and peanut butter play dough at the center. To complete a recording sheet, have a child read the picture clues and answer each question by coloring a thumbs-up or a thumbs-down. Then have her copy the name of her favorite dough in the box at the bottom of the page.

Dough You Know?

Tickle your youngsters' sense of touch and reinforce dough differences with this activity. Gather small samples of modeling clay, play dough, and peanut butter play dough. Out of students' view, place one of the samples in a small paper bag. Review the descriptive charts made in "Dough Differences"; then invite a child to place her hand inside the bag, feel the dough, and guess which one it is.

49

Dough Descriptions

Use this activity to help students see how yeast transforms bread dough into a fluffy, tasty treat. To begin, make a copy of the class chart on page 54. (If desired, use a photocopier to enlarge the chart.) Gather the materials listed and then follow the steps below.

Materials needed:
1 package of frozen yeast bread dough (slightly thawed)
plastic wrap
1 personalized aluminum tart pan per child
instant camera
stapler

Steps:
1. Provide each child with a small amount of dough in a personalized tart pan. Wrap two small dough balls in plastic wrap and freeze for later use in "Warm Risers" (below).
2. Direct students to examine their dough; then record their observations in the left column on the chart.
3. Take an instant photo of one child's dough and then staple the photograph to the left column on the class chart.
4. Cover each child's pan with plastic wrap and place it in a warm area to rise.
5. Remove the plastic wrap from the pan and have each child observe the change in her dough.
6. Record students' observations in the middle column of the chart; then staple an instant photo of one child's risen dough to the bottom of the column.
7. Bake the dough balls for a few minutes less than directed on the package. Let the bread cool; then take an instant photo of one child's baked bread.
8. Have each child examine her bread. Record students' observations in the right column on the chart. Staple the photo of the bread to the bottom of the column.
9. As students munch on their bread, have them review the completed chart and discuss the changes they observed.

This Is Why

Yeast feeds on the sugars in the bread dough, enabling the yeast to grow and produce carbon dioxide gas. Yeast needs warm temperatures to grow and produce gas. The gas causes the dough to expand, or rise.

Warm Risers

Try this simple experiment to show your students how temperature affects the yeast in bread dough. In advance, thaw the two dough balls from "Dough Descriptions" (above). Place each ball on a separate aluminum pie pan and then cover each one with plastic wrap. Show the pans of dough to your students. Then place one pan in the refrigerator and the other pan in a warm area. Later, remove the refrigerated dough and place the two pans side by side. Ask students to compare the size and shape of the dough balls. Then have your youngsters brainstorm reasons why the refrigerated dough did not rise. Guide students to conclude that the temperature in the refrigerator was too cold for the yeast in the bread to grow.

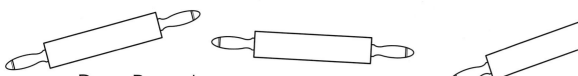

Dear Parent,

We are learning all about dough! Here is a sample to knead, squish, and roll with your child. If you would like to make some more dough, simply follow the recipe below!

Materials needed:
2 c. flour
$^1/_2$ c. iodized salt
$^3/_4$ c. water
mixing bowl
large spoon
cookie sheet (optional)
cookie cutters (optional)
aluminum foil (optional)
craft paint (optional)
paintbrushes (optional)

Steps:
1. Mix all the ingredients in a bowl until smooth.
2. Knead the dough until it is rubbery.
3. Help your child shape the dough into figures, or roll it out flat and use cookie cutters.
4. If desired, place the creations on a foil-lined cookie sheet and bake them at 300° for 1$^1/_2$ hours. Remove them from the oven and allow them to cool. Then use craft paint to decorate them.
5. Store leftover dough in an airtight container or in a resealable plastic bag.

(staple the bag of dough here)

Note to the teacher: Use with "Home Learning Lab" on page 48.

51

Baked Dough

Before the dough is baked it looks...

After the dough is baked it looks...

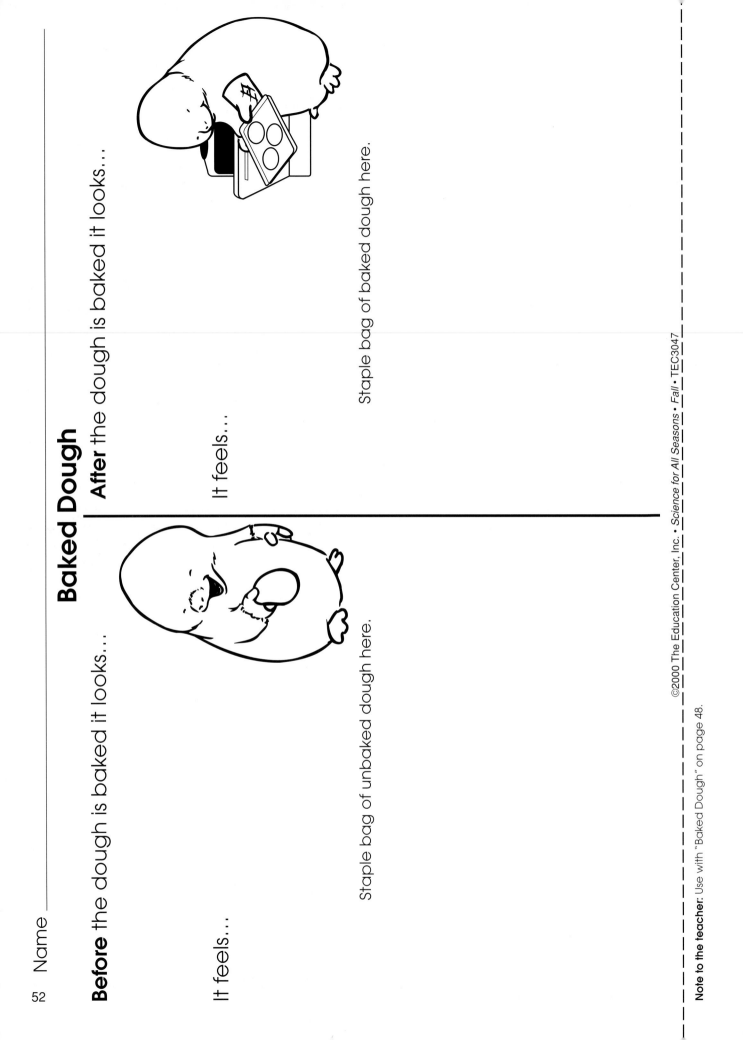

It feels...

It feels...

Staple bag of unbaked dough here.

Staple bag of baked dough here.

Note to the teacher: Use with "Baked Dough" on page 48.

Name _____

Thumbs-Up! Thumbs-Down!

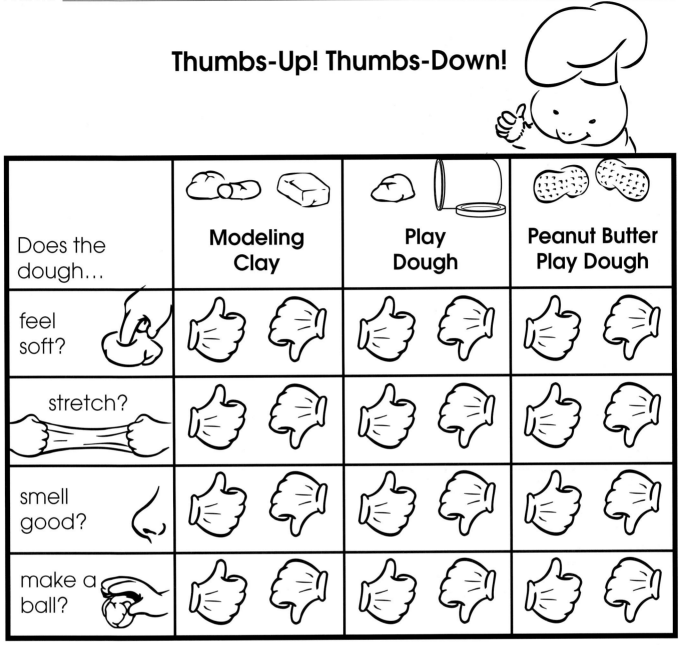

Does the dough...	Modeling Clay		Play Dough		Peanut Butter Play Dough	
feel soft?	👍	👎	👍	👎	👍	👎
stretch?	👍	👎	👍	👎	👍	👎
smell good?	👍	👎	👍	👎	👍	👎
make a ball?	👍	👎	👍	👎	👍	👎

My favorite dough is...

Yeast Dough Descriptions

Before Rising the dough is:	After Rising the dough is:	After Baking the dough is:
(staple photo here)	(staple photo here)	(staple photo here)

©2000 The Education Center, Inc. • *Science for All Seasons* • *Fall* • TEC3047

Note to the teacher: Use with "Dough Descriptions" on page 50.

Energize With Exercise

Encourage your students to exercise the right to have strong, flexible, and fit bodies with these energizing activities!

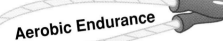
Aerobic Endurance

Recess Exercise

One of the most important elements of a well-rounded fitness program is aerobic exercise. So set your youngsters on the path to fitness with this recess activity that promotes aerobics. After an outdoor recess period, have students discuss the things they did. Explain that some recess activities are *aerobic* exercises for the body. *Aerobic* means with air or oxygen. During aerobic exercise, the heart and lungs work harder to bring more oxygen to the body. Guide your youngsters to brainstorm recess activities that can be aerobic, such as running or jumping rope. Then write the activities on a graph. Over the next several days, encourage each child to engage in one of the activities during recess. After each recess period, invite each child to place a sticker on the graph to show which activity he chose. After a few days, tally the graph to determine which was the most popular activity.

Recess Exercise		
jumping rope	running	tag

Did You Know?

The heart is a muscle! When we participate in aerobic exercise, we use whole muscle groups over an extended period of time. The heart beats more strongly in order to provide more blood to the other muscles at work. Aerobic exercise can strengthen many muscles, including the heart!

Follow the Leader to Fitness

Continue to promote aerobic endurance with this vigorous version of Follow the Leader. To begin, review the information in "Did You Know?" above. Then ask students to list aerobic activities or action words, such as run, jump, and skip. Record the words on chart paper, and then point to each word as one child demonstrates the action. Next, have students form a circle and then appoint a leader to stand in the center. Ask the leader to choose one movement for each child to perform *in place*. Then have students follow the action of the leader for one minute. Allow students to rest for 30 seconds. Continue one-minute exercise intervals with different leaders. Add a little pep to each step with the following chant: "[Jumping, jumping], yes siree! That's the exercise for me!" At the end of the activity, have students place their hands on their chests and try to feel their heartbeats. Are their little tickers thumping?

Flexible Fitness

In addition to aerobic activity, flexibility is another important component of fitness. Use this activity to stretch your little ones' muscles while stretching their minds! To begin, explain to students that our muscles are made of fibers that can be stretched, almost like elastic. Before stretching these fibers, it is important to slowly warm up the muscles. Lead your students in a warm-up activity, such as marching in place for a few minutes; then demonstrate a variety of stretching exercises. As your little ones stretch with you, encourage them to perform the movements slowly and avoid bouncing motions.

After stretching, help illustrate the importance of a warm-up with this activity. Give each child a chilled piece of caramel or Bit•O•Honey® candy and ask her to try to stretch it. Next, instruct her to roll the candy between both palms to warm it. Then have her try to stretch it again. Compare the ease of stretching the warmed candy to the muscles' ability to stretch after a warm-up activity.

This Is Why

Warm-up activities increase the blood flow to the muscles and make them easier to stretch. Regularly stretching our muscles helps keep them healthy.

Building Muscle

Step Right Up!

Your students will march their way to stronger muscles with this small-group stepping exercise. In advance, visit a local health club and ask to borrow a few aerobic stepping blocks. To begin the activity, explain to students that another element of fitness is building strong muscles. Explain that climbing stairs helps strengthen the heart *and* builds strong lower-body muscles. Then have each child in a small group stand close to the front of a step. Instruct her to step up and stop, and then step down and stop. Ask her to practice slowly stepping up and down until she gets the feel for the movement. Then gradually pick up the pace. As students are stepping, have them try to identify which muscles are working. (Don't forget the heart muscle!) When students have mastered stepping, have them sound off the chant below as they exercise on the step.

If we work out every day,
    we'll be strong in every way!
Step up.
One, two!
Step up.
Three, four!
Step up.
One, two,
Three, four!

Did You Know?

Stepping up makes leg muscles stronger because they lift the body up onto the step. Strong muscles are less prone to injury.

I Can Be Fit! Booklet

Have each child create his own guidelines for physical fitness with this booklet. To make one booklet, copy pages 58, 59, and 60. Use an X-acto® knife to cut along the dotted circles on each booklet page. Cut apart the booklet pages. Stack the pages in order; then staple them along the top. Tape a child's school picture behind the circle cutout on booklet page 5. Read through the directions below and gather the needed materials. Then help each child complete his booklet according to the directions.

Cover: Color the cover; then write your name on the space provided.

Page 1: Write a word for an aerobic activity (such as *run, jump,* or *skip*) on the line. Then draw yourself doing that activity.

Page 2: Write the word *stretch* in the space provided. Then draw yourself stretching.

Page 3: Write a word for a strength-building activity (climbing, biking) in the space provided. Then draw a picture of yourself doing that activity.

Page 4: Write your favorite fitness activity on the line. Then draw a picture of yourself doing that activity.

Page 5: Draw a picture of yourself. Then write three fitness activities that you like to do.

Fitness Finale

For a grand fitness finale, set up an exercise course that includes activities to build muscle flexibility, aerobic endurance, and muscle strength. To prepare, set up three playground or gymnasium workout stations. (See suggestions below.) Then have adult volunteers supervise each station. To begin, lead your youngsters in a warm-up activity and a stretching session. Then divide your class into three groups and assign each one to a different station. Have each group perform the activities at the station; then have the group try to guess whether the activities are aerobic, flexibility, or muscle-building activities. When each group has completed each station, have students walk a lap around the playground or gym to cool down.

runner's stretch

quadricep stretch

Aerobic Station
- jumping rope
- jogging in place
- jumping jacks

Strength Station
- push-ups
- lifting one-pound hand weights or unopened soup cans
- squats

Flexibility Station
- toe touch
- runner's stretch
- quadricep stretch

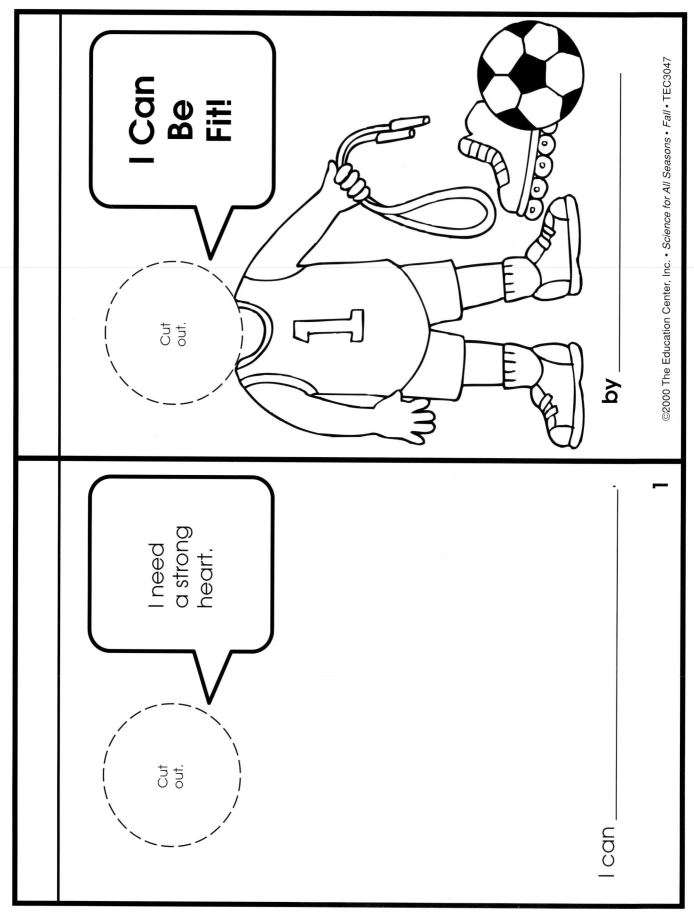

I Can Be Fit!

Cut out.

by _____

©2000 The Education Center, Inc. • *Science for All Seasons* • *Fall* • TEC3047

I need a strong heart.

Cut out.

1

I can _____

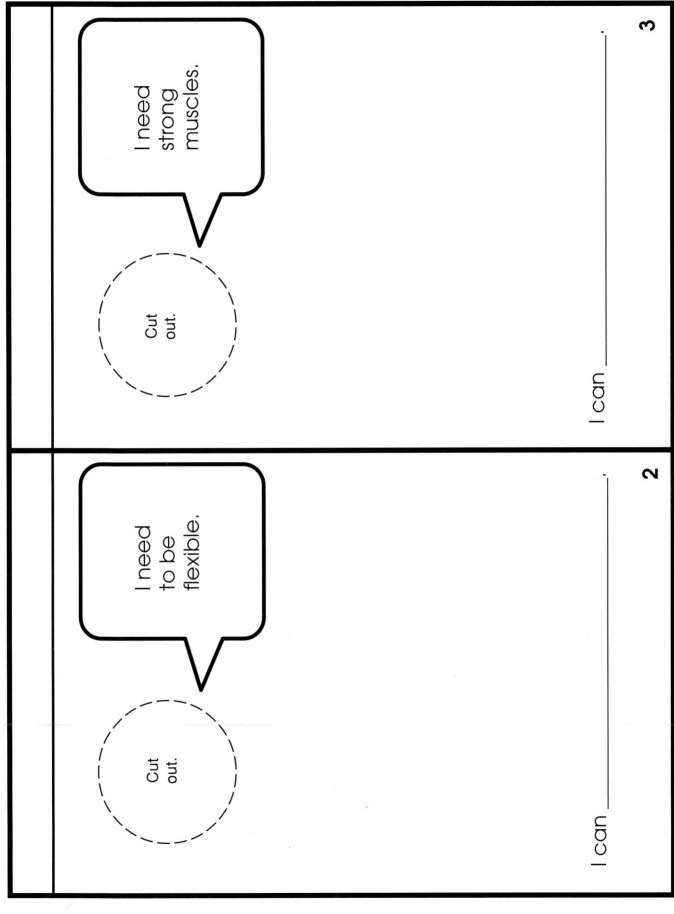

3

I need strong muscles.

Cut out.

I can _____

2

I need to be flexible.

Cut out.

I can _____

Booklet Pages 4 and 5

Use with "I Can Be Fit! Booklet" on page 57.

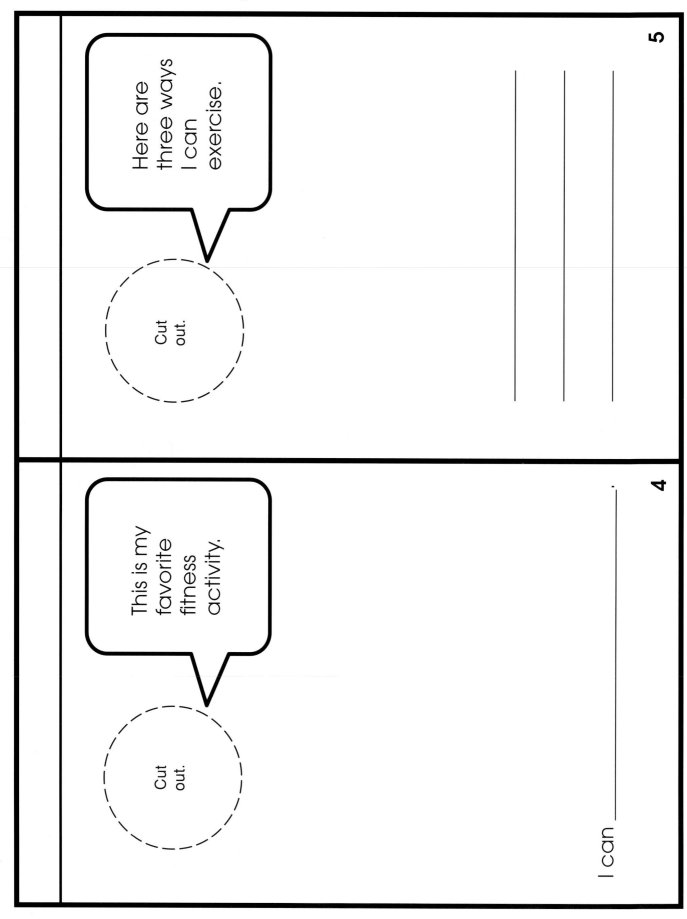

5

Here are three ways I can exercise.

Cut out.

4

This is my favorite fitness activity.

Cut out.

I can _____

Science Highlights

Calling All Balls!

You can bounce it, throw it, catch it, kick it, and roll it.
What is it? It's a ball!

Have a Ball!

Strengthen your youngsters' observation skills with this discovery activity! In advance, put a large ball in a black plastic trash bag and tie the bag shut. Have each student predict what might be in the bag. Next, have him feel the object through the bag and then make a guess. Reveal the bag's contents and initiate a discussion on the properties of the ball. Then arrange your students in a circle and pass around a variety of balls. Have students discuss ways that the balls are alike and different. Then call out a ball characteristic, such as rough, brown, or light. Instruct each student to roll his ball to another child when he hears a word that describes his ball. Continue playing until each child has had a turn to roll a ball.

Ball Characteristics

Your little ones will be moving and singing as they discover what balls can do! Sing the song to the right as your students pass a ball around the circle. After each verse, the child with the ball uses it to complete the action. Balls sure are "un-ball-ievable"!

(sung to the tune of "Pop Goes the Weasel")

Balls can be heavy or light.
They can be smooth or rough.
So many colors they can be.
Roll the ball to me!

Balls are used for many things.
They can be kicked or tossed.
So many colors they can be.
Toss the ball to me!

Balls can spin and roll and bounce.
They can be big or small.
So many colors they can be.
Bounce the ball to me!

61

Behind the Bounce

Your little ones will bounce right into fun with this lively experiment! In advance, purchase two deflated beach balls at a discount store or an end-of-summer sale. Inflate one ball. Have each student take a turn bouncing the inflated ball. Then invite each child, in turn, to try bouncing the deflated ball. Encourage students to brainstorm reasons why only the inflated ball bounced. Your youngsters will be amazed to find out that air is behind all that bounce!

This Is Why

An inflated ball bounces well because it has enough air inside to push its walls outward. When the ball hits a hard surface, the side of the ball flattens against the air inside. If there is enough air inside the ball, it will push the side of the ball back out, making the ball bounce.

Other Balls That Bounce

Introduce your little ones to balls that bounce for reasons other than air! In advance, gather several small solid rubber balls. Explain to your students that not all balls bounce because of air. Pass around the rubber balls and encourage each child to squeeze and bounce one of the balls. Invite each child to guess what is inside the ball that makes it bounce. Then explain that the ball is made of solid rubber. When the ball hits the ground, the side of it flattens against the rubber inside. The rubber inside then pushes the side of the ball back out, making it bounce.

Up in the Air

Amaze your little ones with this ball experiment involving air! In advance, place a plastic funnel and a Ping-Pong® ball at a center. Have each student put the ball inside the funnel as shown. Instruct her to blow downward onto the ball to see what happens. Then have her put her finger over the smaller opening and try blowing again. The ball moves! Invite your little scientists to brainstorm reasons why the ball moves.

This Is Why

When the small opening of the funnel is blocked, air flows around the ball and is trapped in the bottom of the funnel. The trapped air then pushes upward and moves the ball.

Round and Round It Goes

This interactive ball booklet will have your little ones practicing their positional word skills. To make one booklet, duplicate the booklet cover, pages, and patterns on pages 66, 67, and 68. Have a child cut out each pattern, find the booklet page with the matching shape, and then glue the pattern onto the shape. Next, have the child personalize the cover and draw a self-portrait on booklet page 4. Direct the child to color and cut apart her booklet pages; then help her stack the pages in order and staple them along the left-hand side.

To make the movable ball for the booklet, cut a small circle from tagboard. Punch a hole in the top of the ball. Tie a ten-inch length of string through the hole; then tape one end of the string to the back of the booklet. Where will the ball go? Nobody knows!

Kyra's Ball

Round and round it goes. Where it will bounce, nobody knows!

Beside the dog, 1

in front of the tree, 2

under the bridge, 3

and over me! 4

From Here to There

Your students' scientific knowledge will be on a roll with this center activity. To prepare, place a supply of straws, a Ping-Pong® ball, a large Styrofoam® ball, and a golf ball at a table. Tell each student that he will be blowing air through a straw to try to move each ball across the table. Invite the child to predict which ball will be the hardest to move; then have him conduct his investigation. He may be surprised to find that the golf ball required the most air to get rolling. Lead him to conclude that the golf ball was the hardest to move because it was the heaviest of the three balls. Roll, ball, roll!

Home Learning Lab

Count on this activity to strengthen the home-school connection! In advance, duplicate page 69 for each student. Send home a copy with each child and invite her to discover what kinds of balls—and how many—she has at home. Instruct each student to bring her most unusual ball to school along with the recording sheet. Have students compare the variety of balls. Then have them discuss their home findings. Record the results on a chart or graph. Compare, count, and then celebrate!

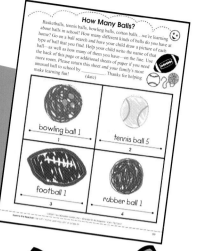

Ball Museum

Encourage your students to focus on the properties of different balls by setting up a classroom museum. Use the balls from "Home Learning Lab" and put them on a table in your dramatic-play area. Invite your students to brainstorm ball categories—such as silliest, fuzziest, or biggest—and then have them create labels to match the categories. Have students vote for each category. Then display the winning balls next to their labels. Encourage students to make admission tickets, signs, and tour guide badges for the museum. Let the tours begin!

biggest

most stitches

best bounce

silliest

Rolling Along

Your youngsters will be amazed to find that different surfaces affect a rolling ball. Have each student experiment with an assortment of balls (Ping-Pong® balls, small rubber balls, Wiffle® balls, etc.). First, have him roll each type of ball on a grassy area. Then have him roll the balls on a sidewalk or a hard surface. Discuss each student's observations. Then have your group brainstorm why a ball rolls better on certain surfaces!

This Is Why

When a moving object touches another object, *friction* is created. A ball rolling over a grassy surface will move slowly because there is more friction. A ball rolling over a flat, smooth surface creates less friction, and therefore the ball rolls farther and faster.

64

Which Rolls Faster?

Involve your little ones in some further investigation of rolling balls. To prepare, gather a large and a small ball, such as a beach ball and a golf ball. Then make a ramp by taping a large piece of cardboard to the seat of a chair as shown. To begin the activity, provide each child with a copy of the record sheet on page 70. Have students examine the balls and predict which one might reach the bottom of the ramp first. Invite two students to each hold a ball at the top of the ramp and then release the balls at the same time. Have each child record the results of the test by drawing a smiley face in the appropriate box on his record sheet. Repeat the experiment, each time having students record the results on their sheets. Lead students to conclude that both balls rolled at the same speed. Amazing!

This Is Why

Gravity causes both balls to roll at the same rate. Their speed does not depend on their size or weight. Therefore, a large ball will reach the bottom of the ramp at the same time as a small ball.

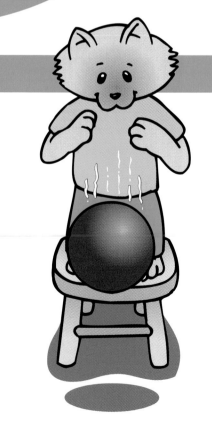

Drop the Ball!

Use this simple experiment to reinforce the effect of gravity on a falling ball. To begin, provide each child with a copy of the recording sheet on page 70. Next, have two students stand on a chair. (For safety, have an adult supervise this activity.) Provide one child with a large ball and one child with a smaller ball. Have the two students hold the balls at an equal height and then drop them at the same time. Direct your youngsters to observe the balls to see if one falls to the ground faster. Then have each child record the results by drawing a smiley face in the appropriate column on his recording sheet. Repeat the experiment four more times; then have students analyze the results on their sheets. Your youngsters will see that once again, both balls drop at the same speed!

_____'s
Ball

Round and round it goes. Where it will bounce, nobody knows!

©2000 The Education Center, Inc. • *Science for All Seasons* • *Fall* • TEC3047

Beside the dog,

1

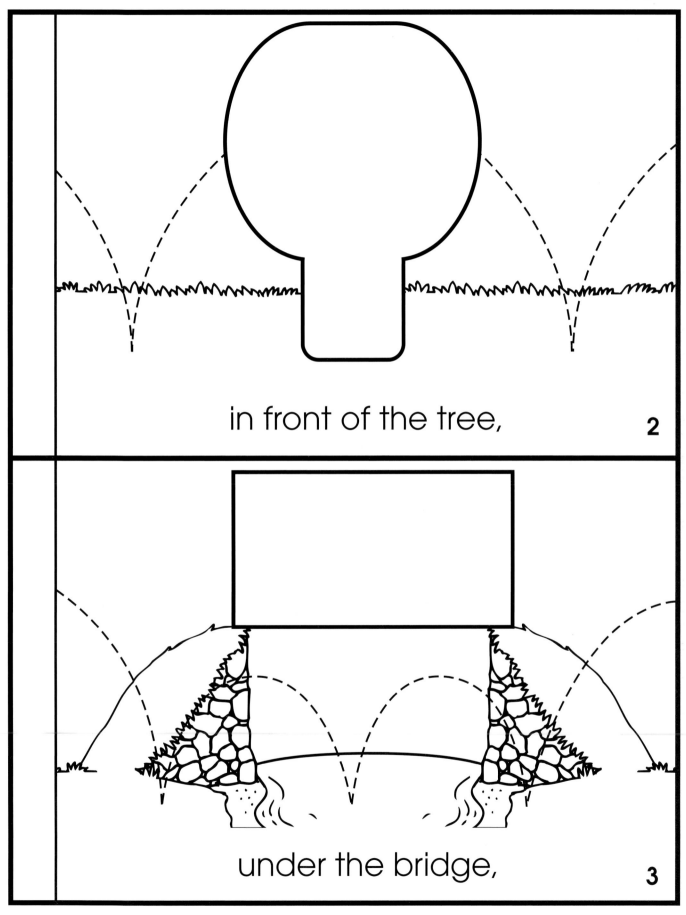

in front of the tree,

2

under the bridge,

3

Booklet Page 4
Use with "Round and Round It Goes" on page 63.

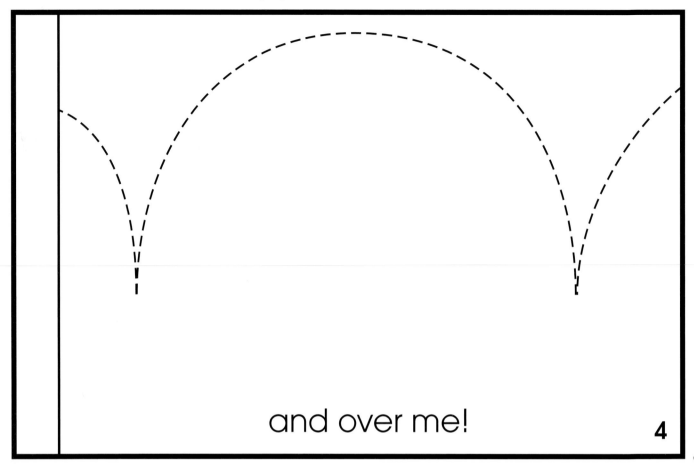

and over me!

4

Booklet Patterns
Use with "Round and Round It Goes" on page 63.

How Many Balls?

Basketballs, tennis balls, bowling balls, cotton balls…we're learning about balls in school! How many different kinds of balls do you have at home? Go on a ball search and have your child draw a picture of each type of ball that you find. Help your child write the name of that ball—as well as how many of them you have—on the line. Use the back of this page or additional sheets of paper if you need more room. Please return this sheet and your family's most unusual ball to school by _____. Thanks for helping make learning fun!

(date)

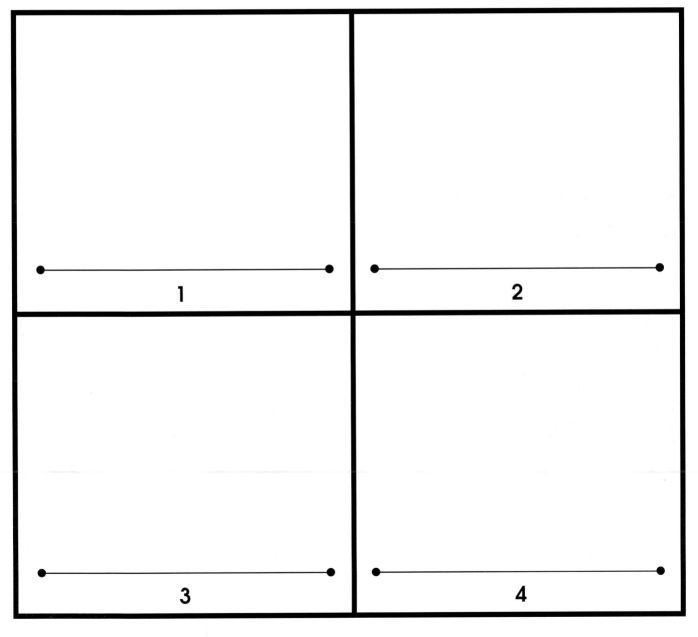

1

2

3

4

Note to the teacher: Use with "Home Learning Lab" on page 64.

Name_____

Which Ball Wins?

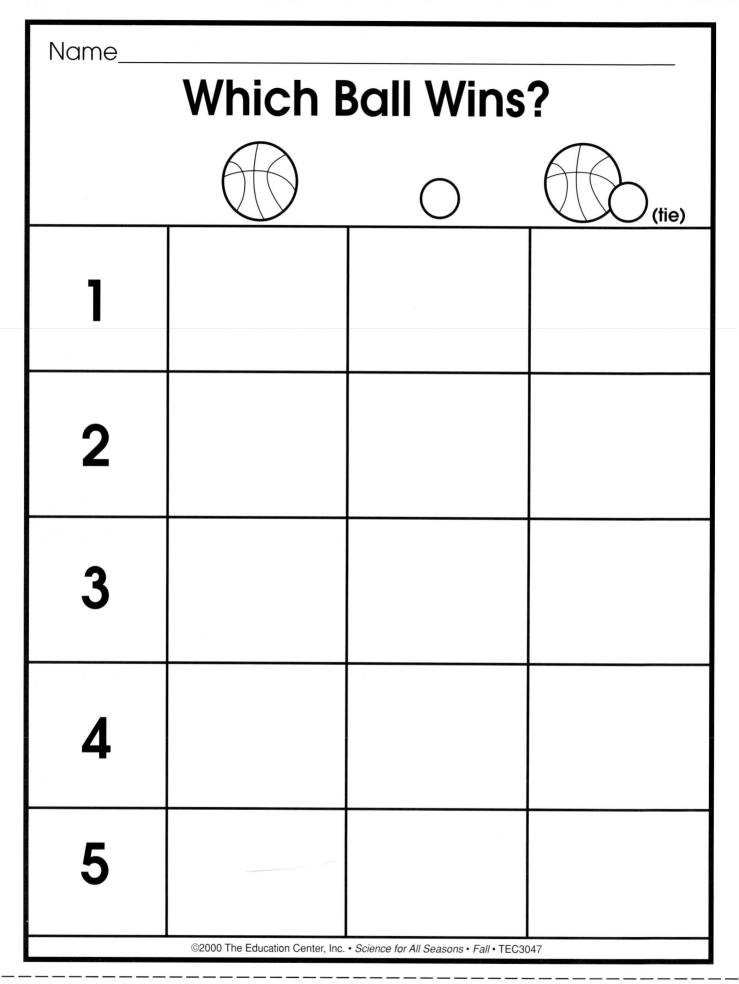

	🏀	⚪	🏀⚪ (tie)
1			
2			
3			
4			
5			

Note to the teacher: Use with "Which Rolls Faster?" and "Drop the Ball!" on page 65.

Water Power

These water activities will whisk you and your students away on a wild and wonderful learning experience!

It's Raining!

Get your youngsters moving in the right direction with this erosion activity. In advance, put a thin layer of sand in your exploration table (or in a large plastic tub). Make a rain sprinkler by punching several holes in the bottom of a Styrofoam® cup. Place the sprinkler at your exploration table, along with a small plastic pitcher filled with water. Invite one student in a small group to form a mound of sand at the table. Then have another child hold the sprinkler directly over the mound as you pour water through the sprinkler. Encourage your students to discuss their observations. Then explain that rain sometimes moves loose sand or soil and that the process is called *erosion*.

This Is Why

When it rains over sand or soil, only some of the water is absorbed. The excess water flows downhill, carrying loose sand or soil with it. This process is called erosion.

No More Erosion!

Your students will feel like scientific experts as they experiment with preventing erosion. In advance, cut several squares of green tissue paper to represent grass and gather a small supply of pebbles. To begin, have a small group of students predict what might happen if rain falls on a mountain of sand covered with grass. Then invite a student to build a mound of sand at the exploration table. Have another child press the tissue paper squares on top of the mound so that all parts of the squares are touching the sand. Have a child use the rain sprinklers from "It's Raining!" (above) to sprinkle water over the mound. Have students discuss their observations; then have them predict what might happen if rain fell on a pebble-covered mountain of sand. Repeat the activity using the pebbles. After this experiment, your youngsters will understand that erosion *can* be prevented!

This Is Why

Plants, rocks, and trees help stop erosion by holding the soil in place.

71

On the Move

Make way for water with this outdoor activity. To prepare, duplicate the reporting sheets on page 75 to make a class supply. Gather the materials listed; then follow the steps below to perform this water energy experiment.

Materials needed:
one 6" x 8" piece of cardboard for each child (Cereal box panels work well.)
two 2-liter bottles filled with water
cookie sheet
1 bucket of soil
1 pencil per child
2 wooden blocks
access to scissors
access to a stapler

Steps:
1. Have each student cut her reporting sheets apart, stack them, and then staple them onto a cardboard back.
2. Take students outside with the needed materials.
3. Have student volunteers cover the back of the cookie sheet with a thin layer of soil.
4. Use a block to raise one end of the cookie sheet; then have a student slowly pour water down the cookie sheet in an even, steady stream.
5. Direct each student to make a sketch of the results on her first reporting sheet.
6. Repeat the experiment, using two blocks to raise one end of the cookie sheet.
7. Instruct each student to record the results on her second reporting sheet.

This Is Why

The higher the cookie sheet is raised, the faster the water flows, giving it more energy. The more energy water has, the more soil it can move.

Sing a Song of Erosion

Reinforce the concept of erosion with this catchy song! In advance, duplicate the patterns on page 76. Color the patterns. Cut them out and then laminate them for durability. Back each pattern with a piece of magnetic tape. (Or use felt for a flannelboard.) As you sing the song below with your students, have a child point to each pattern when it is mentioned in the song. Drip, drop!

(sung to the tune of "Five Little Ducks")

Here's some soil lying on a hill.
Here's a rain cloud ready to spill.
When the rain hit the soil, then the soil did say,
"Rain on a hillside carries me away, me away, me away!
Rain on a hillside carries me away!"

Moving Power

Your little hydrologists will have a blast moving an object with only water power! In advance, stock a center with a plastic tub of water, a turkey baster, and a lasagna pan with a Ping-Pong® ball in it. Have a child visit the center and fill the baster with water. Then have him aim the tip of the baster at the ball and then squeeze the bulb. Challenge him to refill the baster and move the ball using only water power. No hands allowed!

This Is Why

When the baster bulb is squeezed, the water inside is forced out. The force is enough to move the Ping-Pong ball. Other examples of water power include moving leaves with a hose and using the force of water to clean a sidewalk.

Get Carried Away!

Ensure a downpour of fun in your classroom with this booklet-making activity! To make one booklet, duplicate the booklet cover and text strips on page 77. Cut apart the text strips and glue each one to the bottom of a 5" x 7" sheet of construction paper. Read through the directions below and gather the necessary materials. Then have a child follow the directions to complete each booklet page. Help him stack the pages in order and then staple them behind the booklet cover.

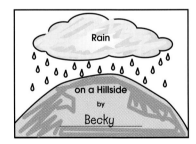

Cover: Write your name on the line. Color the picture.

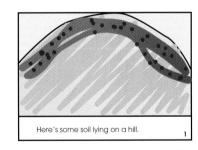

Here's some soil lying on a hill. 1

Page 1: Draw and color a hill. Glue coffee grounds on the hill to represent soil.

Here's a rain cloud ready to spill. 2

Page 2: Draw a cloud on another sheet of paper. Color it gray; then cut it out. Glue it to the booklet page.

When the rain hit the soil, then the soil did say, 3

Page 3: Draw a cloud and raindrops above a hill. Glue coffee grounds on the hill.

"Rain on a hillside carries me away!" 4

Page 4: Draw and color a hill. Glue coffee grounds at the bottom of the hill to represent soil that was washed away.

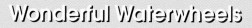

Wonderful Waterwheels

Put a spin on learning with this waterwheel activity. To make one waterwheel, use a sharpened pencil to poke a hole through the center of a three-inch Styrofoam® ball. Then insert a bamboo skewer through the hole. For safety, use masking tape to cover both ends of the skewer. Next, help a child insert four wooden craft spoons into the ball as shown. Sing the song below with your class as each child takes a turn holding her waterwheel under running water. Your youngsters will be amazed to discover that water can turn their waterwheels. Wow, that's power!

(sung to the tune of "The Wheels on the Bus")

My waterwheel goes round and round,
Round and round, round and round.
My waterwheel goes round and round
When water hits the spoons.

Let's Make Waves!

Discover the wonder of water with your child by learning how waves are made!

1. Fill a bowl half full with water.
2. Wait until the water is perfectly still.
3. Hold one end of the straw close to the water.
4. Gently blow through the straw.
5. Try blowing harder.

What Happened?
The energy of the moving air is transferred to the water when you blow through the straw. The energy pushes up the water, forming a wave. As the energy travels through the water, many waves appear.

Home Learning Lab

Strengthen the home-school connection with this simple wave-making activity. In advance, duplicate page 78 to make a class supply. Have each youngster put a bendable straw in a snack-sized resealable bag. Staple the bag to his page. Then explain to your students that they are going to use their straws to make water waves at home. Rippling waves coming up!

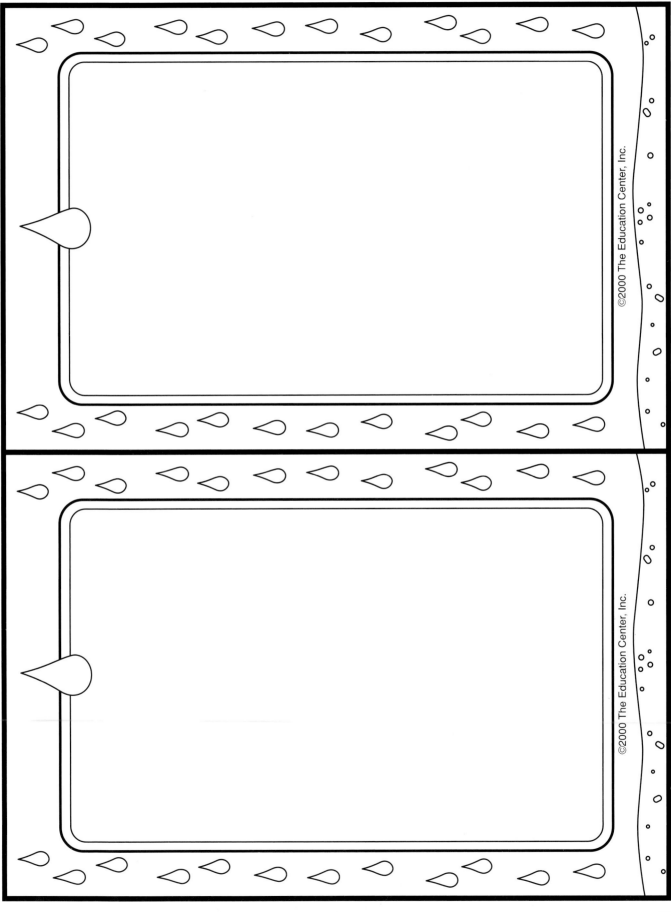

©2000 The Education Center, Inc.

©2000 The Education Center, Inc.

Magnetic Board Patterns
Use with "Sing a Song of Erosion" on page 72.

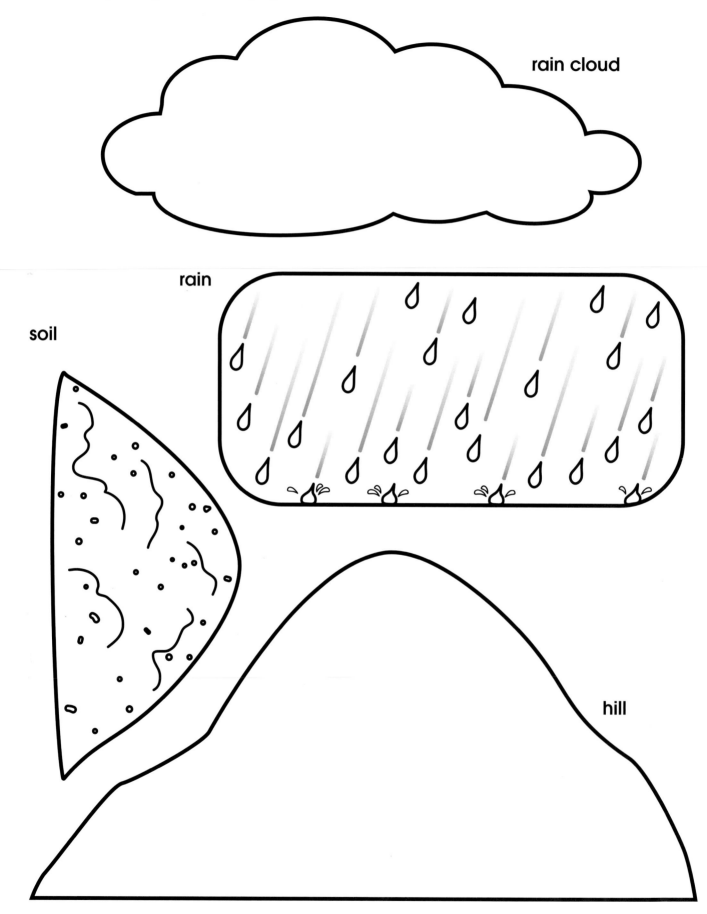

rain cloud

rain

soil

hill

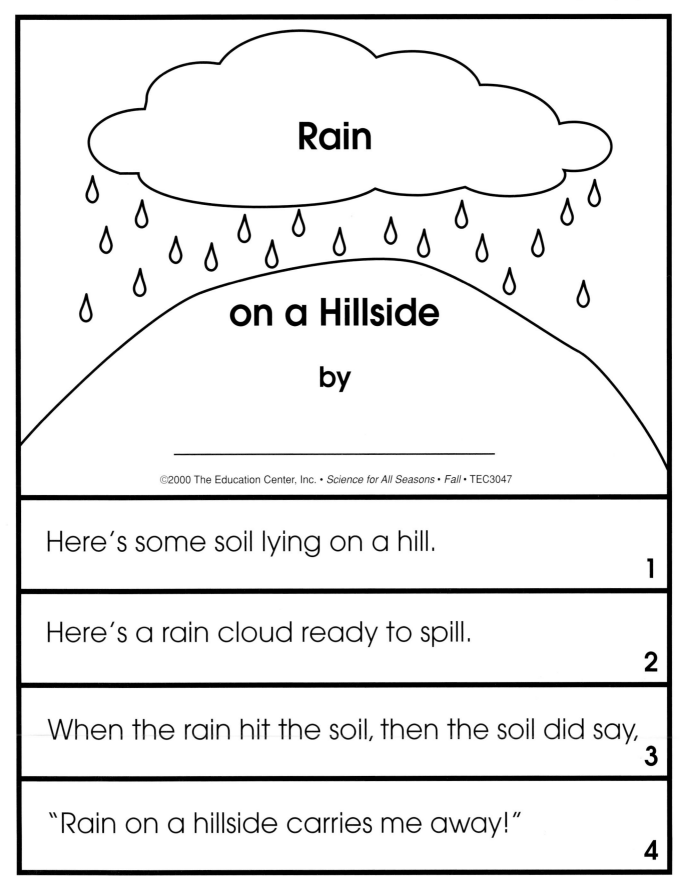

Rain

on a Hillside

by

_____

©2000 The Education Center, Inc. • *Science for All Seasons* • *Fall* • TEC3047

Here's some soil lying on a hill.

1

Here's a rain cloud ready to spill.

2

When the rain hit the soil, then the soil did say,

3

"Rain on a hillside carries me away!"

4

Let's Make Waves!

Discover the wonder of water with your child by learning how waves are made!

1. Fill a bowl half full with water.

2. Wait until the water is perfectly still.

3. Hold one end of the straw close to the water.

4. Gently blow through the straw.

5. Try blowing harder.

What Happened?

The energy of the moving air is transferred to the water when you blow through the straw. The energy pushes up the water, forming a wave. As the energy travels through the water, many waves appear.

- -

(Staple the resealable bag here.)

©2000 The Education Center, Inc. • *Science for All Seasons* • *Fall* • TEC3047

Note to the teacher: Use with "Home Learning Lab" on page 74.

Color Quest

Fall is the perfect season to set your youngsters on a quest for color discoveries.

Lots of Colored Leaves

Kick off your color quest with a study of vivid autumn leaves. To prepare, gather a supply of red, orange, yellow, and green leaves. If leaves are not available, cut colorful leaf shapes from construction paper. During your circle time, have students sort the leaves by color. Next, divide students into four groups. Provide each group with a set of sorted leaves and a large sheet of paper that is the same color as the leaves. Direct the group to glue the leaves onto the paper; then write the appropriate color word on the paper. Display these leafy banners in your classroom throughout your color study.

yellow

orange

A Song of Colored Leaves

Reinforce color recognition with this song and movement activity. In advance, cut out and laminate construction paper leaves in a variety of fall colors. Next, have students stand in a circle, and provide each child with one leaf. Invite students to join you in singing the song below. When a color word is mentioned, encourage students with leaves of that color to move the leaves as if they are falling toward the ground.

(sung to the tune of "Clementine")

Lots of leaves in lots of colors,
Lots of colors all around.
Can you see the pretty [red] leaves?
See the [red] leaves falling down.

Repeat, substituting other appropriate color words for the underlined word.

Leaves of Green

Before they were red, yellow, orange and brown, most of those fall leaves were green! Set up this simple color-mixing center and have little ones create leaves as green as can be. To prepare, stock a center with yellow and blue food coloring, a few spray bottles filled with water, foil pie pans, and a supply of white coffee filters. Direct each child at the center to place a coffee filter in a pie pan. Then have him spray the filter with water until it is damp, but not soaked. Next, have the child squeeze three drops of yellow food coloring in the center of his filter. Then direct him to squeeze a drop of blue food coloring in the center of each yellow spot. To thoroughly mix the yellow and blue coloring, have the child spray his filter with a little more water. Encourage him to discuss any changes he observes. As an extension, invite the child to create different shades of green by experimenting with different amounts of yellow and blue food coloring. When the filters have dried, help the child cut leaf shapes from the filters. Then have him glue the leaves onto a piece of black construction paper.

Did You Know?

Green leaves get their color from a substance called *chlorophyll*. The chlorophyll helps leaves convert sunlight energy into a kind of sugar that provides food for the tree.

Did You Know?

Most leaves are *always* yellow and orange red! The green chlorophyll masks these other colors. In the fall, the leaves stop producing chlorophyll, and the yellow and orange red pigments are revealed.

Mixing Red and Yellow

When most leaves stop producing chlorophyll in the fall, they begin to change colors. Give your youngsters another color-changing experience with this activity. To begin, provide each child with a white construction paper leaf cutout. Help the child fold her leaf in half and then unfold it. Next, direct her to squirt several drops of yellow paint on one half and several drops of red paint on the other half. Have the child refold her leaf and gently rub the outside to mix the paint. Invite your little one to predict what will happen to the paint; then have her unfold the leaf. Encourage the child to carefully examine the paint; then lead her to conclude that wherever the red and yellow paint mixed together, orange paint formed.

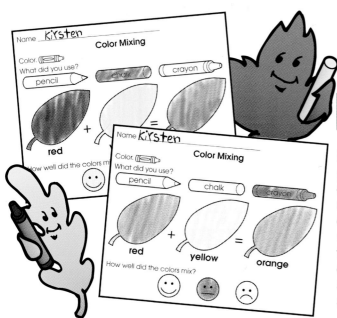

Pencils, Crayons, or Chalk?

Use this small-group investigation to find out which medium will blend colors the best: colored pencils, crayons, or chalk. To prepare, make three copies of the data sheet on page 84 for each child. Then provide each child in the group with the following: red and yellow crayons, red and yellow pieces of chalk, red and yellow colored pencils, and three data sheets. Have students recall the results from "Mixing Red and Yellow" on page 80. Invite each child to predict how well each medium will blend colors; then have her complete a data sheet for each medium. Compare the results of all three investigations and have your youngsters decide which artistic medium blended colors the best!

All Mixed Up!

Here's another interesting way for your crowd to investigate colorful mixtures. To prepare, fill two small clear plastic containers with water. Place several drops of red and yellow food coloring in one container and then stir the water until it turns orange. Next, place several red and yellow sequins in the second container and then stir the water. Your little ones may be surprised to find that the sequins do not change the color of the water.

This Is Why

The red and yellow food coloring mixed with the water and formed a new orange solution. The sequins did not combine with the water and form a new solution. Therefore, the color of the water did not change.

Purple Leaves?

Believe it or not, plants with purple leaves do exist! Several species of flowering plum trees have purple leaves that range in color from reddish purple to purple black. The *coleus* and the *dark opal basil* plants also have pretty purple foliage. If desired, find pictures of these purple plants in garden books and catalogs to show your youngsters. Then prepare for this positively purple activity!

To begin, provide each child with a sheet of fingerpaint paper. Then place a spoonful each of red and blue fingerpaint on the paper. Review the results from "Mixing Red and Yellow" on page 80; then lead students to conclude that mixing red and blue will create purple. Invite each of your little ones to use his fingers to mix the paint, and encourage him to discuss his observations. When the paint is dry, help the child cut leaf shapes from the paper.

Leaf Overlays

Have each child make this handy tool to help herself recall which combinations of primary colors (red, yellow, and blue) make which secondary colors (green, orange, and purple). To make one, you will need sheets of red, blue, and yellow acetate. (If colored acetate is not available, use clear acetate and red, blue, and yellow permanent markers.) Use the pattern on page 84 to make a tagboard leaf tracer. Then use the tracer to cut a leaf shape from each sheet of acetate. Provide a child with the acetate leaves, a small paper plate, and a paper fastener. Help the child punch a hole at the bottom of each leaf; then use the fastener to attach the leaves to the center of the plate. Direct the child to move one leaf over another to reveal a secondary color. For added reinforcement, have each little one use this leafy tool when singing the songs below.

(sung to the tune of "Head, Shoulders, Knees, and Toes")

Blue and yellow will make green,
Will make green!
Blue and yellow will make green,
Will make green!
The finest shade of green you've ever seen!
Blue and yellow will make green,
Will make green!

(sung to the tune of "Row, Row, Row Your Boat")

Red, red, red, and blue
Will make a purple hue.
Red and blue will mix to make
Purple through and through!

(sung to the tune of "Clementine")

Red and yellow
Will make orange
When you mix them all about!
Mix the red in with the yellow,
And some orange will come out!

Color Blending by the Book

Your little ones will love leafing through this booklet that reinforces color-mixing concepts. To make one booklet, photocopy pages 85, 86, and 87 on white paper. Next, use the leaf tracer from "Leaf Overlays" (page 82) to make two red tissue paper leaves, two yellow tissue paper leaves, and two light blue tissue paper leaves. Have a child follow the directions below to complete the booklet pages. When the pages are completed, help the child cut them apart, stack them in order, and then staple them along the left side.

Cover: Write your name on the line. Color the leaf.

Page 1: Use a crayon to color one leaf red, one leaf yellow, and one leaf blue.

Page 2: Brush water-thinned glue inside the leaf outlines. Place a blue tissue paper leaf on one outline. Place a red tissue paper leaf on the other outline. Brush a little more glue over the leaves until the colors in the middle begin to blend. Fill in the blank.

Page 3: Use red and yellow tissue paper leaves, and repeat the directions for page 2.

Page 4: Use blue and yellow tissue paper leaves, and repeat the directions for page 2.

Page 5: Use a crayon to color each leaf to match the color word below it.

A Leaf of Many Colors

Your color-smart students have explored the individual colors found in heaps of leaves. Now challenge each child to discover just how many colors he can find in a single leaf. In advance, duplicate the recording sheet on page 88 for each child. Then gather fall leaves that each contain different colors, such as green and yellow. If desired, laminate the leaves for durability. Place the leaves at a center along with the data sheets, a supply of crayons, and several plastic magnifying glasses. Invite each child to visit the center, choose a leaf, and then use a magnifying glass to examine it. Encourage the child to communicate her observations by completing a data sheet. What a vivid way to wrap up your color quest!

Data Sheet
Use with "Pencils, Crayons, or Chalk?" on page 81.

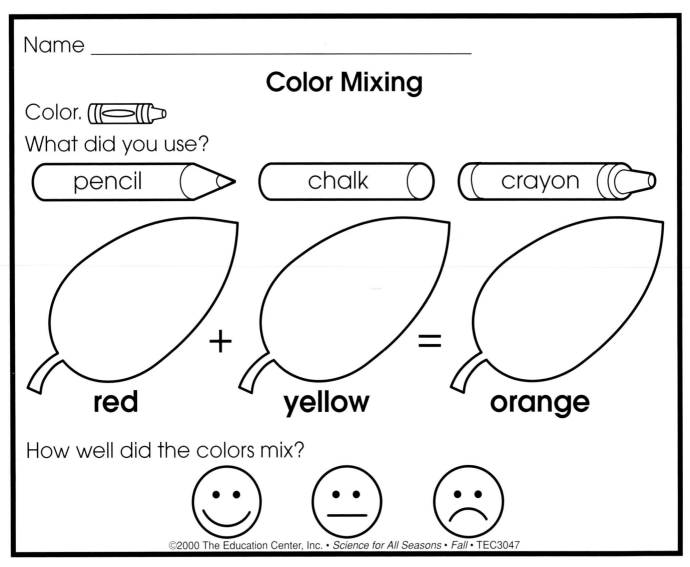

Name _____

Color Mixing

Color.

What did you use?

pencil   chalk   crayon

red   +   yellow   =   orange

How well did the colors mix?

Leaf Pattern
Use with "Leaf Overlays" on page 82 and "Color Blending by the Book" on page 83.

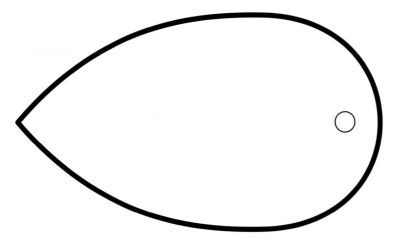

I Can Mix
Colors

by

_____

1

Red, yellow, and blue.

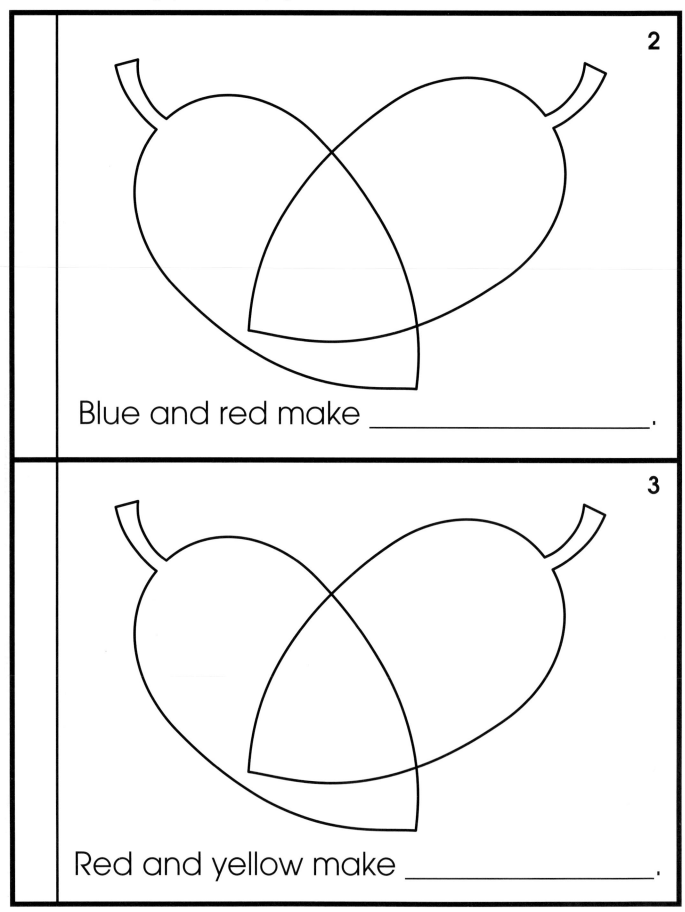

2

Blue and red make _____.

3

Red and yellow make _____.

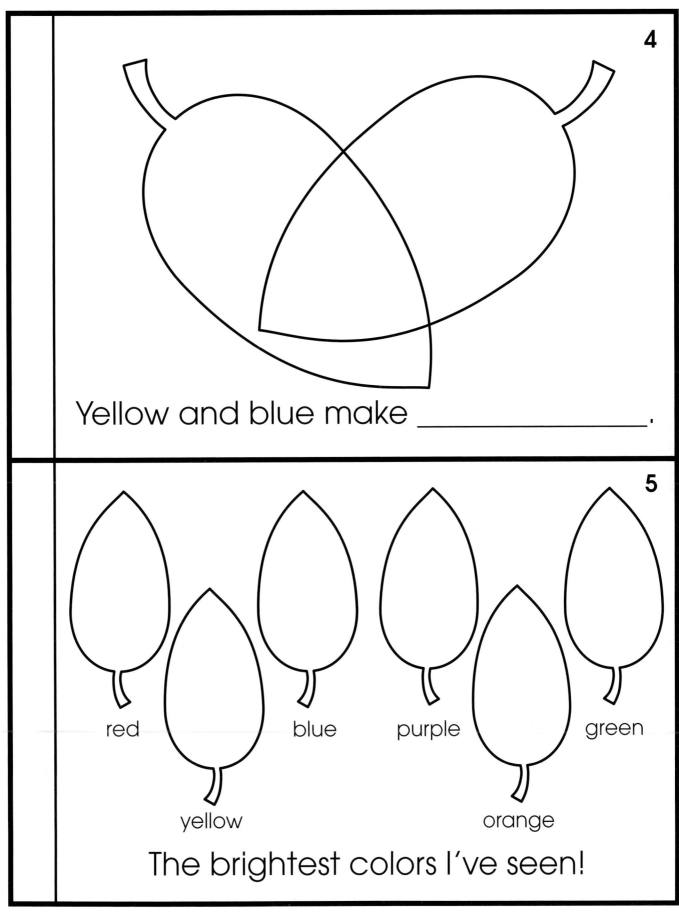

4

Yellow and blue make _____.

5

red   blue   purple   green

yellow   orange

The brightest colors I've seen!

Name _____

A Leaf of Many Colors

✏️ Trace your leaf.

Which colors do you see in your leaf?

🖍️ Color.

(green) (yellow) (red) (orange) (brown)

🖍️ Color your leaf picture.

Note to the teacher: Use with "A Leaf of Many Colors" on page 83.

Kitchen Sink Science

"Boo-tiful" Brews

Stir up some scientific fun with these unique experiments!

Fizzy Fun

Here's a bubbly brew that will have your little ones bobbing up and down with excitement! Have each student place several colored popcorn kernels or Indian-corn kernels in a clear eight-ounce plastic cup; then have the child half-fill the cup with water. Next, have him put one tablespoon of baking soda into his cup and stir until the baking soda dissolves. Invite the child to predict what will happen when vinegar is added to the mixture. Then instruct him to place three tablespoons of vinegar to the cup and observe what happens to the kernels in the fizzy liquid. As a finishing touch, sing the song below with your youngsters to reinforce what they learned. Fizz, fizz!

(sung to the tune of "Five Little Ducks")

First, pour the water in a cup.
Next, add the soda to fill it up.
When you add the vinegar, bubbles brew.
The popcorn kernels dance in the stew,
Fizzy stew, fizzy brew.
The popcorn kernels dance in the stew!

This Is Why

When baking soda is combined with vinegar, carbon dioxide gas bubbles are formed. These bubbles cling to the kernels, causing them to rise. When the bubbles burst, the kernels sink to the bottom of the cup.

More Fun With Fizz!

These booklets are a great way for your scientists to apply their knowledge at home! In advance, duplicate pages 93, 94, and 95 to make a class supply. Read through the directions below and then gather the necessary materials. Next, have each child follow the directions to complete her booklet pages. Then have her cut the pages apart, stack them in order, and then staple them along the left side.

Cover: Color the kernels. Print your name on the line. Color the page.
Page 1: Color the kernels. Draw water in the cup.
Page 2: Color the kernels. Draw water in the cup; then glue some baking soda onto the spoon.
Page 3: Color the kernels. Use a yellow crayon to draw vinegar on each spoon. Draw water and bubbles in the cup.
Page 4: Draw water and bubbles on the cup. Draw corn kernels on the bubbles.
Page 5: Draw water and bubbles on the cup. Glue popcorn kernels onto the page to show what happens.

The popcorn kernels dance in the stew, fizzy stew, fizzy brew,

4

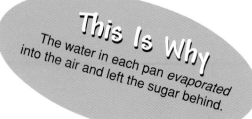

Baking Soda

Sugar Surprise

Introduce your little scientists to the concept of evaporation with this simple sugar experiment! Put two teaspoons of water into a small clear plastic cup. Then stir in ten teaspoons of sugar until the sugar has dissolved. Next, place two teaspoons of the mixture into a foil pie pan. Use food coloring to tint the sugar mixture in the pan. Repeat the previous two steps three more times, using a different color each time. Then place the pans in a warm, sunny area and encourage students to brainstorm what they think will happen to the mixtures. In approximately one week, students will be amazed to see that the water disappeared, leaving only colored sugar crystals in the pan. Surprise!

This Is Why
The water in each pan evaporated into the air and left the sugar behind.

Fizzy Fun!

Discover what salt water can do with this simple—and magical—science activity!

Materials Needed:
2 eggs
2 clear plastic jars (big enough for the egg to fit inside)
warm water
salt
teaspoon

Directions:
1. Half-fill each jar with water.
2. Help your child count and place ten heaping teaspoons of salt into one of the jars. Stir.
3. Try floating an egg in each jar.
4. What happens?

This Is Why
The egg sinks in the fresh water because the egg is heavier than the water. It floats in the salt water because it is lighter than the salt water. Salt water is denser than fresh water. That's why it's easier for you to float in the ocean than in a swimming pool!

Now Try This!
Mix one teaspoon of salt into a jar of fresh water. Then test the egg to see if it will float. How many teaspoons of salt will it take to make the egg float?

Home Learning Lab

This home-based exploration idea will amaze both students and parents! Duplicate page 96 to make a class supply; then send home a copy with each child. After students have had a chance to try the experiment with their families, gather your youngsters and have them discuss their home discoveries about salt water!

"Ink-credible" Ink

Heat up some science magic with this activity that reveals the mystery of invisible ink! Have each child in a small group use water and a cotton swab to draw a picture (or print a message) on one-half of a sheet of manila paper. Next, have him draw a picture on the other half, this time using lemon juice. Encourage students to predict ways of revealing the invisible ink. Then use an iron set on low to warm each student's paper. The lemon juice drawing will turn brown! As an extension activity, have students test a variety of liquids, such as grapefruit juice, apple juice, and ginger ale.

This Is Why
The heat from the iron reacts with the sugar in the liquid and turns it brown.

A Shade of Green

Your little ones will delight in experimenting with a potion that will turn pennies green! Have each student dip a paper towel in a bowl of water and then spread it out flat. Next, instruct her to put three pennies on the towel. Have her fold the towel so that the pennies are covered on all sides and then place the wrapped pennies in a paper cup. Have her repeat the experiment, this time using vinegar in place of the water. Have students brainstorm what they think might happen to the pennies, then let both cups stand overnight. The next day, have each student unwrap her pennies and compare them. Your youngsters will be amazed to find that the vinegar-soaked pennies have turned green!

This Is Why

The copper in the pennies combines with the acid in the vinegar, which turns the pennies green. The water-soaked pennies do not change.

Colorful Concoctions

These natural-dye projects will brighten up your autumn classroom! For each child, cut two leaf shapes from inexpensive white cotton fabric. Have students brainstorm ways to make dyes. Then enlist their help in preparing some natural dyes. In one shallow pan, have a student mix one-half cup of prepared mustard and four cups of warm water. In another shallow pan, have a different child mix one quart of grape juice and one-half cup of cranberry juice. Have students predict what color their leaves might become if they submerged them in each dye color. Then use the directions below to have each student make two autumn-colored leaves. (If desired, have each child wear gloves and a smock to protect fingers and clothes from stains.)

1. Put your leaf in the pan.
2. Wait at least one minute.
3. Remove your leaf. Gently squeeze out the excess dye.
4. Allow your leaf to dry.

Fizzy Stew

by _____

First, pour the water in a cup.

1

Next, add the soda to fill it up.

2

When you add the vinegar, bubbles brew.

3

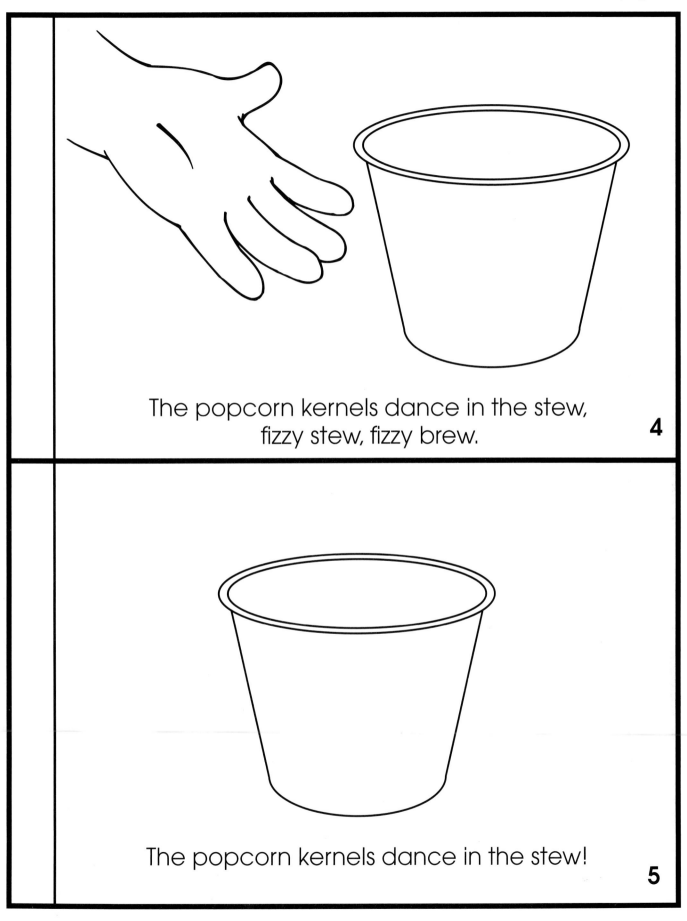

The popcorn kernels dance in the stew, fizzy stew, fizzy brew.

4

The popcorn kernels dance in the stew!

5

Fizzy Fun!

Discover what salt water can do with this simple—and magical—science activity!

Materials Needed:
2 eggs
2 clear plastic jars (big enough for the egg to fit inside)
warm water
salt
teaspoon

Directions:
1. Half-fill each jar with water.
2. Help your child count and place ten heaping teaspoons of salt into one of the jars. Stir.
3. Try floating an egg in each jar.
4. What happens?

This Is Why

The egg sinks in the fresh water because the egg is heavier than the water. It floats in the salt water because it is lighter than the salt water. Salt water is denser than fresh water. That's why it's easier for you to float in the ocean than in a swimming pool!

Now Try This!

Mix one teaspoon of salt into a jar of fresh water. Then test the egg to see if it will float. How many teaspoons of salt will it take to make the egg float?

©2000 The Education Center, Inc. • *Science for All Seasons* • Fall • TEC3047

96   **Note to the teacher:** Use with "Home Learning Lab" on page 91.